WITE OUT

Love and Work

A memoir with poems

OTHER BOOKS BY LINDA NORTON

Hesitation Kit, 2007 (EtherDome)
The Public Gardens: Poems and History, 2011 (Pressed Wafer)
Dark White, 2019 (Omertá)

WITE OUT

Love and Work

A memoir with poems

■

Linda Norton

Hanging Loose Press
Brooklyn, New York

Published by Hanging Loose Press, 231 Wyckoff Street, Brooklyn, New York
11217-2208. All rights reserved. No part of this book may be reproduced
without the publisher's written permission, except for brief quotations in reviews.

www.hangingloosepress.com

Printed in the United States of America 10 9 8 7 6 5 4 3 2 1

Hanging Loose Press thanks the Literature Program of the New York State
Council on the Arts for a grant in support of this project.

Cover art: Linda Norton
Book design: Nanako Inoue

ISBN 978-1-934909-62-1

She is in the dark,
sewing, stringing notes together with invisible thread.
That's a feminine accomplishment:
a feat of memory, a managed
repletion or resplendence.

Rae Armantrout

So will my page be colored that I write?
Being me, it will not be white.

Langston Hughes

CONTENTS

CONTENTS

Dark White

We have one mother and some fathers, we come from clan. O the poverty of our identity, to be so proud of what we guess we are. I am a church of that. Of such weightless stone I build my plinth, with color alone.

—Robert Kelly, from "Berlin Sonnets"

1

Flying out of Boston after a literature conference in Cambridge. Theory, theory, theory, and a professor rhapsodizing about spanking. And there was a talk about the amygdala. ("The amygdala receives inputs from all senses as well as visceral inputs.")

The plane leaving Logan swooped low over the South Shore; when I looked out the window I did a double take—we were passing over the house I grew up in. Ma's laundry was there on the line—her polyester pants, her dish towels. Across the inlet from the back of our house, the shipyard and the Proctor and Gamble stacks. Sometimes, when I was a teenager, the air was so thick with the smell of Ivory Soap, I'd gag. "That's not pollution," Ma would say. "*That's clean.*"

In the ship's manifest for the *Giuseppe Verdi* on which my mother's parents traveled from Palermo to Ellis Island in 1924, there is a column where they note the complexion of each Sicilian immigrant—dark, fair, swarthy, yellow, whatever. This category doesn't appear on the manifests of ships that came from Ireland, like the *Scythia* on which my father's mother arrived from Cobh that same year. There's also a place to note identifying marks on the faces of the Italians from the South; lots of men had scars on their faces.

Anarchists had bombed Salutation Street in the North End and many other targets. Sacco and Vanzetti had been unjustly prosecuted. All Italians were suspect. Most of the Sicilians on the ship *Giuseppe Verdi* were labeled "dark white," but there must have been some question on board about my mother's mother; "fair" is noted, then crossed out.

There's a drawbridge between our house and the shipyard and soap factory. Ma says her father, a cement mason from Salemi, worked on it for the WPA in 1936. He was a tyrant, they say; volcanic.

In Sicily, he and my grandmother grew up near Erice. A volcano and goddesses and work, that's the heritage. When my mother's father was a baby in the province of Trapani, Emily Dickinson was still alive in Amherst ("Vesuvius at home," she called her father), writing New Englandly of Sicily:

> Partake as doth the Bee,
> Abstemiously.
> The Rose is an Estate —
> In Sicily

In my parents' kitchen at sunset, washing the dishes and looking north, I thought the black Ivory smokestacks against the sky were beautiful.

2

When I told my grandmother I was going to visit Chicago, she crossed her arms over her chest and frowned. "Chicago—lotta blacka people!"

My sister laughed and said, "Yeah, Nonie, that's why she wants to go there."

"Oh, stop it, Caroline," I said. But I laughed too.

"Che cosa? Che fai?" Nonie was confused. No capisce.

"Never mind, Nonie."

———

Nonie wanted to tell me something; my mother translated.

> She says that when she came to this country she didn't understand no English and she didn't know no one and my father locked her up in that place in East Boston on the top floor—
>
> She says she heard kids playing in the street and wondered why they weren't working—

2

She says when she was a girl in Salemi all the kids worked. They did piece work, made doll dresses like the ones she crochets for you girls—

She says the boys worked in the salt pans or watched sheep or picked grapes—

She says when her baby brother Nicolo died of cholera she helped her mother dress him in a little suit—

She says it was hard to get his arms into the sleeves—

—

Last year I told my mother the story about Nonie saying, "Lotta blacka people!"

My mother said defensively, "Oh, but Nonie liked some black people."

"What are you talking about? Nonie didn't know any black people."

"Oh, she really liked Tina Turner."

"Are you kidding me?"

"No, I'm serious. Nonie pretended she didn't know no English, but she liked TV. Remember when Tina wrote her book and went on all the shows? Well, all that stuff that she talked about—the things Ike did to her, the beatings—that's what Pa did to Nonie."

3

On my volcano grows the Grass, A meditative spot —

Emily Dickinson, #1677

My daughter at six dreamed she was an "international playboy," though she had no idea what that was. She curled up beside me; I gave her a sip of my juice. I told her what I'd been reading for my reading group: *The Life of Samuel Johnson.*

I didn't tell her about the really white woman in the group who often mentioned her fair skin and famous husband. Reading, I was deciding, was something to do alone or with one other: this little one, my girl.

In bed I told my daughter about Boswell, who listened to everything Samuel Johnson said and wrote it down. She kissed her own hand, thinking it was mine, and wondered aloud, "Who was Boswell's Boswell?"

Fair-minded little Portia, my Isabel with her crooked bangs (I cut them wrong).

She seems so mellow now, but is she? Did she stir inside me as I watched a tantrum on the subway, that boy in fatigues shooting a toy gun at his pregnant mother? "Please take his gun away," I did not say. This was on the F train. I gave up my seat for her though I was also pregnant. But I wasn't visibly anything.

—

Our women were clean, especially the Italians. The Irish said Italians were dirty. In the South End, when my mother was six, my grandmother went to work in a factory, sewing men's uniforms alongside Sicilian, Syrian, and Lebanese immigrants.

We were dark white, but in New England we were immaculate.

Snow made me, I said to summer when I missed the winter.

When it was winter, I burned.

—

Lizzie Borden took her axe
Gave her mother forty whacks
When she saw what she had done
Gave her father forty-one

Bunch of little Catholics in the schoolyard, jumping rope to Yankee gore. "La la la" is one thing sung, another thing in chalk or cursive. In cold type, it has no tongue. We were happy when jumping, didn't mind the drizzle, were too young to bleed or even know about it. The boys played far away, another species. They ran around with sharpened sticks; we chanted murder.

4

Now I know that it was very hot when (they say) Lizzie Borden slaughtered her parents. And she had her period when she did it (did she do it?). And her father had killed her pigeons.

—

My father's people were Irish, and instead of sewing and eating and fighting, they drank and sang and fought.

Packed into the back seat of the car, we belted out:

She had a baby six months old,
Weela weela wallia
She had a baby six months old
Down by the river Salia.

She had a big knife three feet long,
Weela weela wallia
She had a big knife three feet long,
Down by the River Salia.

She stuck the knife in the baby's head,
Weela weela wallia
The more she stabbed it the more it bled
Down by the River Salia.

In our car, even the baby tried to sing it, though he didn't know the words.

—

Driving to the factory outlet in Fall River to get our winter coats, my parents hissing at each other in the front seat, I thought of Lizzie Borden. Maybe her mother told her she smelled. I don't know what her father said. Probably nothing. But she knew he thought she was disgusting. Her parents agreed on this at least.

She was often alone with them. She gorged on biscuits upstairs in a closet, if there were any biscuits. If there was nothing to eat, she sucked a wooden dowel dusted with sugar. She had a thirst for justice, a kind of lust.

Who lives in that house now? Is it covered in aluminum siding like those around it? Oh, no—now I see—it's a B & B.

—

I'd never heard of Emily Dickinson. Jump-rope rhymes were all I knew of poetry. The subject of the poem, the author of the murder. Lizzie Borden had no privacy, no rag or paper of her own. She bled and it was a mess. She heard voices and couldn't get them down.

—

My sister got the blue coat, I got the red: wide-wale corduroy. For a while I was confused about the wale and the whales, Fall River and New Bedford, the garment factories and Melville's ship, and corduroy itself, but now I know: corduroy is, in essence, a ridged form of velvet. You could see the trimmings on the factory floor. I took a scrap of my sister's blue.

4

My international playboy, my daughter, reminds me that she needs some Tampax. In my notebooks from her fourth year, I find a receipt from Bill's Drugs in Berkeley. I bought night diapers for her, Tampax for me, condoms for me, extra strength Tylenol for me, and bobby pins for her, since she was getting too big to swallow and choke on them. I'd never bought condoms before.

—

When Isabel was small she sat in my lap and we looked at a book of paintings from the Met. I told her about the Holy Family, the Trinity, all that. I told her about Christ, but I didn't say he was her savior.

We turned to other nativities. She was fascinated by the baby in every picture.

"Look, Mama, now she's in her crib." "And now she's having milk." "Now the angels see her."

My daughter thought the main character was a girl. I didn't correct her.

—

Then it was Holy Week. On the way home from Our Lady of Lourdes I saw that someone had discarded sheaves of palms on the side of the road. Fr. Seamus Genovese had blessed the palms.

"Oh, what a shame," I said, picking them up.

Isabel asked, "Mom, what is 'shame'?"

Had I somehow raised a child who didn't know what shame was?

—

One Sunday a few years later, we watched a documentary about Pearl Harbor. Isabel started to ask me a question and I knew intuitively what it would be.

"Mom, are there rules in war?"

My heart broke. Someday she'd have to learn about war, rape, death. But this was not that day.

"It's Sunday night," I said, turning the VCR off. "Time to get ready for bed." "But it's not night yet," she said, and she was right. So we discussed all the words for what it really was: dusk, twilight, sunset, evening.

—

At fifteen she was five inches taller than me. One night she helped clean up after dinner, handing me the plates and looking down at me in our tiny kitchen. Then she sat on the couch and we talked about whether or not she could get her nose pierced.

She asked if she could do this for her sixteenth birthday; I told her to research it and make a case for it and let me think about it for a few days.

The next day I stopped at Hee Sook's restaurant. The hostess had a nose piercing. "It's hard to keep clean," she told me. Isabel was disappointed when I told her that I wanted her to wait three months to see if she still wanted the piercing; she wished she had talked to me earlier about this, so the three-month waiting period would have been over by her birthday, October 5th. I started washing dishes. She picked up her homework.

Five minutes later, as I turned to wipe the counter, she looked up at me, stricken.

"What's wrong?" I said.

Tears were running down her face. "It's so sad," she said.

"What? That I won't let you get your nose pierced right away?"

I went over to sit with her on the couch and gave her a hug.

"No," she said, and held up her book. She was reading Plato's apology for Socrates. I asked her to read some of it aloud to me. She wiped her tears and read the part about Socrates, wisdom, god and the gods, and then she lost it.

"They killed him anyway," she sobbed, shaking her head.

—

Last week we were rolling around, wrestling and laughing. When we finished wrestling, we sprawled on the rug, and I felt something in my hair—her bobby pin had migrated.

—

I want to write a book for her about a woman wearing rags between her legs while stitching haberdashery. Soaked through while sewing lapels and buttonholes. A faint fingerprint of blood on the peach-colored lining of a suit. No poems sewn into that lining. No English. But we were there.

And Here We Are in Oakland: Journals

like bitter Henry, full of the death of love,
Cawdor-uneasy, disambitious, mourning
the whole implausible necessary thing.

John Berryman

Having identified the shit
the shit you can't say shit about
that's all I can say about that

Fred Moten

1997

What Mommies Say

And here we are in Oakland, exiled from Berkeley. No one wants to rent to a single mother with a two-year-old in the dot-com boom. This is the only place I could find—a one-bedroom in a six-plex, with one closet and a coin op laundry in a dirt-floor basement. I don't know anyone who lives in Oakland. I had to beg the weird landlord to let us live here. I cried when I signed the lease. How many times over the last fourteen years did I see landlords practically begging my feckless husband to sign a lease, no credit check required, because he's a tall, white, blue-eyed man with a deep voice and an air of entitlement?

When we first moved to Berkeley from New York two years ago, I was in heaven—all the pretty gardens and farmers' markets, and my new job.

But then I noticed the smug liberalism and the whiteness. "Where are all the people?" I asked Andrew. Someone told us we should go to Oakland. Except for working as a waitress at Mavis the Pie Queen in 1986, I'd hardly ever been to Oakland.

One Friday we drove to a Vietnamese place called Le Cheval. The huge dining room was filled with all kinds of people. Everyone smiled at Isabel as I carried her to our table near the bar. "Beautiful baby," said a man in a Raiders cap. "Pretty girl," said a middle-aged woman in a Tupac T-shirt.

"Oh!" I said to Andrew. "Here's where the people are."

—

In the new place, I sat in my only armchair, surrounded by unpacked boxes, with Isabel in my lap. I paged through *The New Yorker*, homesick.

"Talk about that," she said when she saw a picture that she liked.

I nursed her and put her down and went into the kitchen. I thought she was asleep until I heard her murmuring "Mamamamamama." I went in to check on her. She was wide awake. She looked amazed.

"I was just talking about you!" she said—as if it were a coincidence that I walked in just then—as if she'd conjured me.

———

Business trip to New York. First time I've been back since Andrew and I split up. I had to pay for Isabel's ticket because she's more than two years old, no longer what they call "a lap infant." But she spent the whole trip in my lap, playing and crying and nursing and sleeping, and I stared at her face for hours.

We stayed with Leah and Young in their Brooklyn brownstone. Now we've all got little kids and his career is hot and we're all confused by my new status: single and living far away. I can't be as helpful to them as I used to be, or as close to Young. Oh, and I have a new boyfriend.

Kneeling in Young's parlor in Brooklyn in my bathrobe, I bent over Isabel to change her diaper. A dog barked outside, and she said, "Doggies say woof!" I kissed her. "That's right, that's right!" I said. "And what do mommies say?"

In that instant I was almost afraid—I knew her answer would tell me what kind of mother I was.

She smiled and said, "Mommies say, 'It's okay, it's okay.'"

Because everything will be okay.

Tom and Young were in the kitchen whispering. I called out to them, "What's the latest gossip?"

Silence. I stood up with the baby and turned toward them.

"Well," Tom said, "you're pretty much it."

"Me?"

Wow, I thought. Who would have expected it?

———

That night Young and I stayed up late talking and drinking whiskey. I told him about Park. I hadn't cheated on Andrew—I'd waited until we announced our breakup.

"And he's a Buddhist," I said.

"Is he Asian?"

Young was Korean American, and Park could be mistaken for a Korean name, I guess.

"Uh, no. He's a *California* Buddhist.

Young groaned. *"Another* white guy?"

Another white guy. It wasn't as if I'd had a string of them. I'd married young, and I'd been faithful. I'd had a life with boys and men before I met my husband, and it was interesting, but it was so private that I'm not even sure I knew very much about it.

"Let me guess," he said. "Park is tall and has blue eyes."

I laughed. "And he's very handsome."

———

Back in California. It was hard to be married and it's hard not to be married. But now there's no fighting in my house. My child can sleep without hearing her mother scream at her father. I can sleep without hating myself or him. Ideally.

Park comes over on the nights when Isabel is with Andrew. I cry, he comforts me, and then he makes love to me. And then I want him to leave, but I don't say anything. I feel like I've been an imposter among people like him and Andrew—"the better class of people," as my high-school guidance counselor called them—for many years. I'm tired. And I want to go home. But there's no home to go to. That's why I'm here, alone.

———

And never alone. Never not thinking about my daughter. Men seem more and more . . . irrelevant. A distraction from my female paradise.

When Isabel was an infant, she nursed a dozen times a day and was colicky. She screamed and I cried; I was sleep-deprived, loving someone I couldn't please.

But then, when she was about four months old, things changed. I told Erin, "I don't understand—she really loves me."

Erin laughed and said, "That's how it is with babies. They don't know any better."

—

Office politics is a kind of hell. Will I have to leave this job? In the New York office, I worked so independently. I don't know how to play the game here, though I know how to get things done. I seem to be caught in a Bermuda triangle of managers who hate each other. One of them lied about me last week! I found out when Doris in human resources took me aside to warn me. "They smile in your face and stab you in the back." What am I supposed to do with this information? I've been raised to turn the other cheek, but how does that work at work? You're supposed to promote yourself to get promoted here, and I'm not good at that.

I took a day off to go on a field trip with Isabel and the other preschoolers. On the bus to Crab Cove I was so happy. Isabel sat on my lap all the way there, and Grace leaned on my arm. On the way home I let Grace sit on my lap. This is the kind of work I'm good at.

—

Isabel is at Russell Street. We call the houses by their street names. Much better than saying "Mommy's house" and "Daddy's house."

Watching *The 400 Blows*, made the year I was born. "Each time I cried," the narrator says, "my father would imitate me on his fiddle."

—

Letter from Young today. The kids, the art world, travel, marriage, parties, and famous friends, replacing me.

That day, nine years ago, when he called me at my office on 42nd Street to tell me that Leah had been raped and left for dead, half-naked, her arm broken, hair matted and tangled, pants hanging over the edge of the bridge. It was Mother's Day.

A homeless man gave her his shirt. Someone called the police. They took her to the hospital.

"You're the first person I called," he said, and I was surprised. He had so many friends.

She and Young were on shaky ground then, relationship-wise—she'd called an old boyfriend first, but he didn't answer. Then she called Young, who brought her home from the hospital. She sat in a kitchen chair while he painstakingly untangled her hair. A big, sad job.

The police showed her binders filled with pictures of men who might have done it. She didn't see her attacker among them, and she didn't listen to the cop who suggested this or that black man might be the one.

She was on her bike on the way to her waitressing job. She said hi as she passed him. He came after her and hit the back of her head with a pipe.

It was around that time that I started to cook for them once a week. I made cheesy potato casserole and chicken with cream sauce and capers— things she wouldn't usually eat. She could live for days on raspberries and the occasional Power Bar; she was already famous, in our little world, for her steely will, her mighty but delicate femininity, her lack of body fat, and her hair.

Not long after the attack, I was shopping at Pearl Paint. I had started making tiny paintings when I couldn't write, and I needed a tube of titanium white. Real artists like my husband and Young and Leah didn't use much white, but I depended on it. I was looking at the most expensive blue—ultramarine—when I overheard two guys in the next aisle gossiping.

One guy said, "I heard it was a gang rape."

They were talking about Leah. Everyone knew Young and Leah.

The other guy said, excitement in his voice: "Yeah, five black guys!"

I could almost hear them grinning.

But this was all in their minds. It wasn't a gang rape. It was just one guy. And he was black, but Leah never emphasized that.

I left the store without my paint.

—

At home when I'm alone, I read furiously, and write in my notebook.

"Chaos, then, is not a scene of disorder—it is a scene of emerging order." Edward Casey's *The Fate of Place.*

"Anyone who likes to think with a pen in his hand is a writer." Michel Leiris

And anyone who thinks about her losses as much as I do—tries to understand and document them—is either crazy or a writer.

—

But if I'm the writer, why did Andrew, the painter, take the computer?

Because he takes everything. Because I'm not worthy. Because I make do. Like everyone expects me to.

—

This afternoon we made bread and then Isabel "developed" two recipes with yeast, bananas, black-eyed peas, jimmies, and blueberries. She put them in the refrigerator and checked on them every few minutes.

In the farmer's market a florist gave her two irises. Before bed we turned off all the lights, switched on our flashlights, and turned the flowers into shadow puppets.

—

To New York for work. First time I've ever been away from Isabel for so long. I'm still nursing her, and I didn't know if my milk would dry up on the trip. But I have plenty of it, and I squeeze it out of my breasts when I shower here.

Tonight Leah and Young had their weekly dinner party. Leah looked at my chest and said, "Your boobs must be ready to burst." She suggested I nurse her newest baby, Eva (after years of anorexia, Leah suddenly can't seem to stop getting pregnant, and somehow she's thinner than ever). She handed Eva to me. Would this baby take to me? Eva began to suckle so furiously that we laughed. She nursed for a long time while gripping her mother's hair. The babies, the milk, us—Leah's hair now—it was like a dream. The guys kept passing plates down the long wooden table in our direction, trying not to stare.

———

Visited Knopf to negotiate paperback reprint rights for the letters of Wallace Stevens. The next day I came up to Boston on the train. Bob told me to try to meet Jorie in Cambridge but I couldn't schedule it. We talked on the phone, though, and I swear I heard her famous hair brushing the receiver.

Saturn, Jorie said, is now finishing its dark transit.

"Are you a Taurus like me?"

"Yes," I said. "How did you guess?" Poet's intuition, I suppose.

"Have the last few years been hard for you?"

"Incredible," I said, too ashamed to say more than that. I'd have to talk about Icarus to make my situation understood in Harvard Square, and that would be inaccurate and bathetic; Icarus was a classical boy, not a girl from Dorchester.

"Me too," she said. "This has been such a hard time."

She has a student who's the daughter of the Queen's astrologer, so she gets top quality transatlantic advice about the zodiac.

"Dame So-and-So" [I didn't catch the name] "says things will get better for us soon."

Us? Us? Who is this "us"?

—

I checked out of the Charles and went down the South Shore to see my parents and go through boxes we left in their cellar. I found the clock Andrew's rich grandparents gave us for our wedding. It was broken when we got it.

—

We were so young. Andrew was the second or third WASP with whom I ever had a real conversation (my roommate in senior year was the only Protestant at our Catholic college, and a dyke, and I thought she and her parents were wonderful; so rational). I was thrilled to marry a guy who read books and laughed at my jokes and never raised his voice or hit me, and I loved his parents, though, even then, their priorities confused me. They liked Paris and cheese (Stilton and Gjetost) and awards and prizes; and they didn't like kids or want grandchildren.

Andrew's mother had published an essay about her feminism in a book I'd read before I'd ever met her son, so it was if I'd already known her, or at least imagined her. I was flattered by her attention, the new translation of Petrarch and the records that she gave me. But her kind of white feminism required a high-status husband and father to subsidize it, along with staff to handle the drudgery of motherhood. My kind of feminism was all about service. In this way, it was just a version of the Catholicism I thought I was leaving behind.

The first time I visited them in Berkeley, I couldn't believe all the books my in-laws had, including two copies of The Fountainhead. *I'd never heard of it, didn't know how to pronounce the author's name. Was it a man or a woman?*

"Ayn Rand," my father-in-law said. "One of the most important books I've ever read." He was an architect and the protagonist was an archi-

tect, too. I'd never known an architect, or any man so devoted to his
work. I was infatuated with the whole family.

Now, fifteen years later, back in my parents' cellar, I traced my fingertips over my brother Joey's old books. Andrew had reminded me of Joey—a blond snob. Too good for me.

It was getting dark and cold. I climbed the rickety stairs, past my parents' separate stashes of spices, powdered milk, cans of soup, his and hers; hers with notes taped to the lids: "Dick, DON'T touch this!"—"DON'T" underlined five times.

—

Home. Andrew's stepmother Jeannie and father Steven came for dinner on Sunday. They've never been here before. I listened to Sinatra while I cooked and then switched to big bands. I checked the clock and poured some wine and looked up "beguine" in the dictionary and learned that, before it was a dance, it meant "white woman" in the Caribbean.

Isabel woke up from her nap and I picked her up just as the doorbell rang. "Oh, there they are!" I said, and buzzed them in. We waited at the open door as they came up the stairs. My neighbor Spring was leaving her apartment in the back. I saw the startled look on Jeannie's face as she came down the hall—I lived in a building with black people?

"Come in!" I walked them through Isabel's room to the kitchen, which doubles as the parlor.

"Is this the whole place?" Jeannie asked with a strained smile.

Steven boomed, "It's marvelous! Artistic—like something in Greenwich Village!"

I made ravioli with Meyer lemon cream sauce and basilico and salad and raspberries with pomegranate molasses. As we sat down to eat there was a noise.

"What was that?" Jeannie said.

"Oh, nothing," I said, though it sounded like gunfire.

I thanked them for coming all this way.

Steven looks great and keeps up with Jeannie, twenty years his junior. They're like an ad for a retirement investment company. Happy, prosperous, nice teeth, good hair. Aging whitely.

Rain splattered the kitchen windows and Steven burst into song, as he is wont to do, addressing a few bars of "Singin' in the Rain" to Isabel. That deep bass voice pains me now; Andrew sounds just like him.

Over dessert, Steven asked Isabel, "Have you seen the movie?" I nodded. We've watched it on the VCR. "Gene Kelly is the greatest tap dancer in history."

I hesitated, then said, "The greatest *white* tap dancer."

Steven frowned. Was I correcting him?

I let it drop. They're well-intentioned, educated white people, not racists like you see in the infamous Boston neighborhood where I grew up. A distinction without a difference.

They kissed Isabel goodnight, and I felt grateful. As I walked them down the hall, we ran into Spring's son Alex. Steven reflexively touched Jeannie's arm as if to protect her as Alex headed toward the front door, ignoring us.

"Is this a bad area?" Jeannie whispered.

"He lives here," I said, pointing to the door of the apartment behind mine. "That woman you saw when you got here—that's his mother."

Now we were in that "panic-stricken vacuum" about which Baldwin wrote. I know it well—I've been forced to wrestle with it since I was a kid in Boston. Or I forced myself, not knowing what I was doing.

And still not knowing.

Note to self: Look for library books or videos about Honi Coles, Nicholas Brothers, etc., so Isabel can see.

—

When Andrew picked Isabel up today he told me that Jeannie and Steven had never been to Oakland before. It seems there are lots of white people who won't come here. I didn't grow up here, so I didn't know that.

Andrew said they liked the food.

"And they really enjoyed the diversity."

Except for what I learned from waitressing at Mavis's in the '80s, I don't know much about the place I live, or its history. Is it like Roxbury or the South End or Mattapan? Where are the projects here?

—

In Boston when I was a little girl, my aunts and cousins were the last white people in the projects. When we visited them, we passed black people in the hallway. I looked down at the floor, too shy to smile back at even those who smiled at me. I knew what my mother thought about them, and I was ashamed.

On the way over to Franklin Field, passing through black neighborhoods where men sat on the stoops and stood on street corners, Ma always did her Negro impersonation. I wondered why there were so many men in the streets instead of at work. I knew better than to ask my mother. I was beginning to realize she was an unreliable narrator, and I'd have to learn for myself.

When the news came on and they showed police in the South turning their dogs and fire hoses on black protesters, my mother mocked me for taking it too seriously: "Oh, Linda loves the Colored people."

Of course, I didn't actually know any Colored people.

—

Every time we visited my aunt, my mother would tell us: "If she offers you anything to eat, just say no thank you." We didn't know anyone who had a lot of anything, but these cousins (and the others who lived in projects) were actually poor. Their father had disappeared, and my aunt had five kids to feed.

One night when we visited, there was a black boy eating a tuna fish sandwich and watching TV alone in my aunt's crowded parlor. We'd never seen this boy before. He and his mother lived down the hall. His mother had had to go out, and she had no one to watch her son, so she'd asked my aunt for help.

"His mother had an emergency," my aunt said. "She had to go to work."

"'Work'?" Ma said. "Is she a 'working girl'?"

My aunt winked at my mother and they laughed.

I didn't understand. What was the mother's work? Why did she have to go out at night? Was she a nurse?

"Watch what you say in front of this one," my mother said to Auntie Mary, casting a glance at me. "She don't miss a trick."

———

The next time we visited, there was a pile of back issues of Jet *on Auntie Mary's kitchen table. That's how the boy's mother had repaid the favor—with magazines.*

Ma and Mary paged through them at the table.

"Oooga booga," my mother said, reading about the doings of celebrities like Pearl Bailey and Nat King Cole and Sammy Davis Junior.

My mother reached for another magazine on the stack, then dropped it as if she'd burned her hand. I picked it up. It was so old, it was creased and crumbling, but you could still see that awful picture—was that a face? Was it even a person? I turned the pages. It was Emmett Till.

"Put that down," Ma said, reaching back to slap my hand. "That's disgusting."

"He shouldn't a said nothin'." My mother's voice shook. "The mouth on him."

"What kind of mother lets them put a picture like that on the cover of a magazine?" My aunt, one of my favorite people, could be judgmental. "What kind of mother does that to her kid?"

———

Was it that year or the next when the riots began in the projects? We ducked down in the kitchen and peeked out the window to watch the trashcans burn. After that my mother took a new way to Franklin Field, avoiding Blue Hill Avenue, which had "turned," as they used to say. And then we stopped going to the projects altogether.

My aunt and her kids finally got out. They had to leave their furniture behind. It was infested with roaches and she wanted a clean start on the top floor of a triple decker closer to us in St. Mark's parish.

———

Who was that woman who gave my aunt that stack of magazines? What did she do, what did she think, where did she come from? What was her name? What happened to her next? Sometimes I think I will spend my whole life trying to understand that mother, and Emmett Till's mother. And my own mother, and the men who killed Emmett Till, and that lying white woman in the grocery store in Money, Mississippi.

1998

Thank You for Telling Me

In New York again for work. Young and Leah wanted to go to an opening, so I volunteered to mind all the kids (L & H watched Isabel for me today while I went to meetings with publishers in Manhattan).

On the way home from Manhattan I heard church bells playing "My Way." That could only mean one thing: Sinatra was dead.

When I got to Park Slope I turned the radio on and started cooking mac and cheese for the kids. I fed them and then I put them to bed. Then I raided the cabinets and found a dusty bottle of bourbon. I sat next to the radio, sipping and listening to the sounds of Sinatra mingled with reggae blasting from a car downstairs.

Leah and Young got home around eleven. Leah went up to check on the kids and went to bed. Young stayed up to drink and talk with me, like we were trying to sneak our old friendship into all of this new life. After an hour, Eva started crying, and Leah called down to Young. "Just a minute," he said, and he finished his story about the time his mother threw a bunch of hundred-dollar bills at him during an argument.

"Young!" Leah yelled.

I'd never heard her raise her voice before.

He went upstairs. I went to bed. But I couldn't sleep. I got up to look at books I'd bought at Gotham Book Mart. From Gregory Corso's "Marriage"—published the year my parents were married—

and everybody else is married! All the universe married but me!

Ah, yet well I know that were a woman possible as I am possible then marriage would be possible—

—

Back home. Too hard to be away from Isabel. We clung to each other all day. At night when she was falling asleep she said in the dark, "Mom?"

"Yes?"

"Do you remember that time we went to Crab Cove and you let Grace sit on your lap on the bus?"

"Yes."

"I didn't like that."

"Oh, I didn't know that. Thank you for telling me."

She squeezed my hand, smiled, and fell right to sleep.

1999
The Toughest

I let Isabel and Kaela sleep in my bed last night, but they couldn't stop giggling and fooling around, so I went in and lay down between them. "That's enough," I said. "Go to sleep." They were suddenly so still and quiet, I almost burst out laughing in the dark.

Then Isabel whispered across my chest at Kaela: "My mom is the toughest."

—

In the Mission today I stopped to look for Halloween costumes and found some good stuff in a thrift store where everything seemed to come from the closets of men who'd died of AIDS. I think I'll dress up as a king this year.

When I was ten, I made a costume from cardboard and poster paint. I went to the party at the community center on Dix St. as a U.S. mailbox. I had cut the mail slot so I could look out. I was so proud of what I'd made. But during the parade my costume got turned around and I couldn't see where I was going. I was mortified. I haven't really dressed up since.

That was the first time I ever went anywhere without my pack of little siblings. I was so excited. I'd read about independent girl heroines. But individuality was not as fun as I thought it would be.

My mother just could not pronounce the word "costume." She said "cos-troom." She couldn't pronounce "pilgrim," either. She called them "pil-drims." I kept correcting her, to no avail. She said whatever she wanted to say, the way she wanted to say it. English wasn't her mother tongue.

—

I dressed Isabel as a cow for her first night of trick-or-treating ever. When we got to the third or fourth house the lady offered her an Almond Joy. She looked into her bag and said, "No, thank you, I already have one." Child doesn't understand the concept of greed.

—

What to teach her at Christmas when I'm not raising her as a Catholic? I remember when Andrew and I took my sister's son for a walk in Carroll Gardens at Christmas in 1989, when he was five. The Italians in that neighborhood were famously excessive at Christmas, their brownstones decorated with strings of lights and Santa Clauses and elves at the nativity with rein-deer and sheep and angels mixed up together. Stopping at one front yard, Seth said, "Who's that baby next to Santa?" Had Caroline not mentioned Jesus to him at all? I don't think Christmas should be all about Santa.

—

Andrew came upstairs when he dropped Isabel off last night. I'd put some orange tulips in a vase. About my minimal flower arrangement, he said, like a connoisseur, "That shows good breeding." I almost spit out my wine.

"Good breeding? What are you talking about? You knew my parents."

I guess he thought he was giving me a compliment on how far I've come in life.

—

I'm re-reading *Middlemarch*. Those deluded heroines in Eliot and James—they were upper-class, with too much time to think—that's all I could see when I was in college. I couldn't relate to their tragedies. If a marriage wasn't overtly violent, what could be wrong with it? Now I turn the pages and cry as I copy lines into my notebook.

"And then the marriage stays with us like a murder—and everything else is gone."

"Here and there is born a Saint Theresa, foundress of nothing, whose loving heart beats and sobs after an unattained goodness . . ."

—

I never dreamed of having of a coveted job like the one I have now, but how can I manage without a wife to do chores or a husband to pay the rent or parents to help with babysitting and logistics? There are no other single mothers, no broke people, doing acquisitions at any of the university presses.

But this was an amazing day. I met Judy Butler, presented two Knopf reprints at the editorial meeting, and offered a contract for the collected Lorine Niedecker. I'd first read Niedecker when I moved down to New Haven to live with Andrew. The only job I could get was at a book warehouse in East Haven—sad sycamores with the tops cut off lining the bus route. After work, I'd get on the bus and sit with the workers from the cheese factory and the mattress factory. Some of them were developmentally disabled. They called out to each other from the front of the bus to the back while I paged through old issues of *Origin*.

> *right down among em*
> *the folk from whom all poetry flows*
> *and dreadfully much else.*

By the time we got to the New Haven green, a world away, I smelled of cheese, too.

2000
Nobody Says So

Oakland, and the Great Migration, and the Black Panthers, and the blues, and my stack of library books—

"Eddie is white, and we know he is because nobody says so," writes Toni Morrison, re: Hemingway's *To Have and Have Not*, in *Playing in the Dark: Whiteness and the Literary Imagination*.

And Flannery O'Connor, from *Everything That Rises*:

> "The ones I feel sorry for," [the mother] said, "are the ones that are half white. They're tragic."
>
> "Will you skip it?" [said the son]
>
> "Suppose we were half white. We would certainly have mixed feelings."
>
> "I have mixed feelings already," he groaned.

He knows better than she does, but he's still a fool in his self-righteousness.

What, I wonder, is the right way to be white?

———

> "They're animals," my mother would say as we drove through the ghetto on the way to Nonie's.
>
> How she loved to provoke me. And I'd always take the bait.
>
> "Stop it, Ma."
>
> She'd laugh. "Oh, Linda, you're too serious. You think too much!"

———

A father at Isabel's school asked me out in the parking lot last month. Tim is a widower and everyone says those are the best catches as they don't have the baggage of divorce. He's good looking but not my type—

very chiseled, a bit conceited. But he is a former Stegner Fellow and a poet.

A very poetical poet. After the first date he wrote me a poem and I was embarrassed for him. But people seem to think he's nice, and poor him, because his wife died and he has two kids. I'm too hard on men, right? And I don't want to be alone all of my life. (Or do I?)

Did I mention that he's white?

After a few more dinners out, we went to Homestead and my friend Jack waited on us, charming as ever. No wonder everyone thinks of him as the mayor of Lakeshore Avenue. But the more solicitous he was to Tim, the more uncomfortable Tim seemed, and the more he drank. While waiting for dessert, Tim confided that in a way he was happy that his wife had died because they'd been headed toward divorce anyway. I felt the hair on the back of my neck stand up.

He ordered another drink and so did I, and then he ordered a double shot of gin. I was afraid of him driving but it was a short ride to my place and I just wanted to get home.

In the car he asked me if I had said goodbye to "Roscoe." I didn't know what he was talking about and then I realized he meant Jack. I said, "His name is Jack," but he kept muttering "Roscoe" under his breath and laughing. By the time we got to my building I couldn't wait to get out of the car. But Tim didn't like that idea. He parked and insisted that he'd walk me to the door of my building because "this is such a bad neighbor-hood." Then he insisted on walking me upstairs to my apartment. When I said goodnight at the door and tried to close it on him, he pushed it open and laughed in my face. I could smell the gin on his breath.

I pushed him out the door and slammed it and he kept knocking and knocking. Then it was quiet and I thought he was gone. But soon he started throwing rocks at my front window and yelling my name.

I turned off all my lights and sat on my bed in the dark, not knowing what to do. After a while I saw the lights of a police car. Apparently my downstairs neighbors had called the police on him.

The police—one black, one white—came upstairs to see if I was okay. I said I was, and they asked me if I had any children with this guy. I said no, I hardly knew him. I told them I did have a little girl. They told me I should get a restraining order against this guy. And they suggested I tell the people at Isabel's school to watch out for him as he had been talking crazy and was capable of anything.

Two days later he called me to ask me to forgive him. I hung up on him.

On Friday I left work early to go to the Oakland court house to get the restraining order but I didn't have enough money for a process server. Plus what about his kids? His poor motherless kids. Plus everyone thinks he a nice guy. A nice widower.

—

Down on Lakeshore Avenue on Saturday in bright sunshine. African guys in robes and turbans hang out at Peet's every morning. They're very dark and look like royalty in those clothes. Like the three kings visiting the infant Jesus. On Saturday, they sit in the pocket park next to the drug-store and play chess. A light-skinned African-American man walked past and peeked in at their dark faces. "Hey, need a little light in there?" They all laughed. Deep, booming laughter.

—

The life in the street here—the daily daily—

"Her whole body panging and pinging," writes Zora Neale Hurston, "A hippy undulation below the waist that is a sheaf of promises tied with unconscious power. She is acting out, 'I'm a darned sweet woman and you know it.'"

Reading while drinking, writing in the margins—

Notch-bracket-underline

"These little plays by strolling players are acted out daily in a dozen streets in a thousand cities, and no one ever mistakes the meaning."

Notch, notch, notch

2001

Transchieving

"Oh Mom," Isabel said tonight. "Daddy had to come to school today to comb my hair."

"Why? Did they find lice?"

I thought I'd gotten them all the last time I checked.

"No, but I had eggs in my bangs."

———

Waiting in the lobby for the parent-teacher conference with Kadijah the kindergarten teacher. Cold grey day after cold dark night.

Mary Ann and Rod come downstairs from the classroom. They are beaming.

"Oh, isn't Kadijah wonderful!"

"She's great, yes."

Kadijah and I went out for drinks last week when our girls were with their fathers. In a school where all the teachers wear sensible shoes, Kadijah wears boots with spiked heels and gets down on the floor with the kids. We all love Kadijah.

"But this epidemic of lice!" Mary Ann says.

"Oh, it's terrible," I say, scratching my head.

Big-boned Mary Ann clutches Rod's arm. He's a grinning patriot who loves George Bush and looks just like Al Gore.

Mary Ann purrs, "Rod and I check each other's hair for lice every night. I just don't know how you single mothers handle this alone."

"Yeah," I say, "it's tough."

She talks about their kitchen renovation and their upcoming vacation at a Mexican resort.

"Rod found a school near the resort where he volunteers as an inspiration-al speaker when we visit."

She wears matching outfits and smells like air freshener. Imagine her pitying me for having no Rod of my own!

I smiled and nodded and went up to see Khadijah.

And all day long I nursed a grudge. I should have said, "Oh, it's OK, Mary Ann. These days, when Isabel's at her father's house for the night, I go down to Kingman's, I pick up some guy, and I tell him, 'Take me from behind and check me for lice.'"

———

Bad dream last week: my father grinning at me, toothless. His God loves him. But who loves me?

That day he got all of his rotten teeth pulled in one afternoon at the VA—it was my job to help with his bloody gauze while he moaned. That was one of the few times I was ever alone with them without the other kids. Ma drove us home over the Mystic River Bridge.

"Dick, Dick, Dick," she nagged. "The dentist told you not to do it all at once."

He couldn't afford to miss another day of work, and she knew that. Now he had to wait for his gums to heal before he could put in the dentures.

He was forty-four.

———

On the phone my brother Richard says he's waiting for all his plans "to come to fruitition." Like our mother, he is inventive with the language. Neither of them has had the kind of formal education that cramps your style. Years ago, she got a restraining order against him, but now that he's medicated he's allowed in her kitchen once in a while. He can do his laundry there, but he has to pay them. It never ends well. He tries to explain to our mother that parents are supposed to love their children unconditionally. He saw it on Oprah. "Hey, Ma," he says. "You watch

Oprah, don't you? How about a little unconditional love, Ma?" She laughs in his face.

———

I write to Michael to ask for a reality check about Richard. He writes back:

> *He is who he is. He gets riled. It can be jarring, but I don't let it upset me anymore and I practically embrace it now. Things seem illogical but I don't try to persuade him, and he's very smart. I learn from him. I go with it. It's okay, even fun a lot of times. He coined a new word that I love:* transchieve. *It's when you transcend and achieve simultaneously. Isn't that a tremendous word?*

Michael takes the ferry from Hingham to Boston every morning and walks through the Boston Common to his job at the State House. He says that some days, when the weather is especially miserable, Richard will be waiting at the ferry in his cab to give him a ride. They don't see each other much. Michael has never been inside Richard's place in Chelsea. He and his beautiful wife keep their distance from Richard and from me, too, now that I'm a single mother like my sister. That's how it is. Michael is the only shining thing. The rest of us are damaged or dead.

———

Recurring nightmare: my sister—eleven months to the day younger than I, and prettier, with blue eyes and dimples—trapped in a dirt pit. I kept reaching down, she kept reaching up. She was screaming, crying. My arm wasn't long enough, I couldn't save her.

Fanny writes about a character with a history of incest: her father had "interfered" with her. Yes, that's the word for it. The things you can't talk about.

In New York, in 1993—seven years after Joey had died and a month after Richard had been sent to Bridgewater State—after my prince of a husband had asked me yet again to pay his share of the rent, his college loans, his taxes—I cracked and went to a therapist, though I didn't

*really believe in therapy, or know how to do it. Since I knew I'd be
downtown on Wednesdays for that appointment, I'd schedule business
lunches immediately afterward, to save carfare and time.*

*One day, right after a session, I walked to the Time Cafe and waited
for Albert, an editor from* The Voice. *Russell Simmons, rap royalty, was
across the room, holding court. The gay man and the pretty woman next
to me were talking about their dysfunctional alcoholic Catholic fami-
lies. They were younger than I, and much better dressed. And they both
hated their oldest siblings.*

*"The superego on them!" she said. "They always 'do what's right.'" Air
quotes. "You know?"*

*"I know!" cried her friend. "It's impossible to imagine anyone ever
wanting to have sex with someone like them."*

*They screamed with laughter. I burst into tears and went into the bath-
room to try to pull myself together. I came out and found Albert waiting
at our table. When the waitress asked me if I wanted a glass of wine, I
said yes, though I never drank during the day.*

———

Andrew brought Isabel to me at the usual time, 5:30 on a Saturday night,
and she sat at the other end of the couch and read her book while I read
Eros the Bittersweet. I trembled slightly in the silence, aware that this was
the first time we had ever read silently together and apart. Arrowed out in
different directions, intimate but separate.

———

My brother Richard is on the phone in his cab in Boston, answering my
call and telling the guy in the backseat: "It's my sister from California."

"Cali-phony-a." Said with relish and a kind of amazement.

"How's the weather there?" he shouts.

"Oh, beautiful. The usual."

Oh, how I wish that it would rain.

"What's it doing there?" I ask.

"It's bitter, Linda. It's wicked bitter."

—

In the office, opening a package postmarked "Bristol / Bath and Taunton," I find a manscript redolent of the smell of a kitchen in England—fish, toast, linoleum, and cigarettes.

I was in the lingerie section at Ross tonight after work, buying underpants, when I felt a huge clot fall out of me. Blood trickled down my legs into my shoes as I heard a man's voice calling me. "Linda, Linda, hello!" I looked up with astonishment to see A. B., the bipolar co-translator of the edition of the Song of Songs that I just published. He was holding a bra and panties on little hangers and walking toward me.

"Abe," I said, "I can't talk to you while I'm shopping for underwear."

"Oh," he said, "I just wanted to tell you why I didn't say hello to you last month at the lecture—it was because you accidentally offended me without meaning to."

"Sorry," I said, "this is not the place or time."

He backed away while I looked down at the blood on my legs and ankles.

Tonight I finished reading *If He Hollers* and started on Himes' autobiography, *My Life of Absurdity*.

Mine, too. Mine too.

—

At my desk yesterday I squeezed my breasts to see if I had anything left. Almost seven years after giving birth, I still get a drop from the left one. It tastes like goat milk.

—

Caroline calls to complain about Ma and Dad and "our divorces."

"I'm not divorced yet," I say.

"Divorced" doesn't seem like something a good girl like me should ever be. And I can't stop using the word "we."

She, on the other hand, is trying to screw her ex for everything he's worth.

(*They were so different, they could have been sisters.*—Frank O'Connor).

"It's great that we're both single," she says. "Now we can both go out with black guys and drive Ma and Dad crazy."

Should I tell her that I'd decided long ago not to play that game? Should I mention my black friends in college? Or that I knew August when he was the cook in the social services agency where I worked, before he ever had a play produced at Yale or on Broadway, and that he'd courted me?

No. I don't talk about him.

But Vee used to say that white people should speak up to white people. So should I speak up now? Say something to my sister about the "black guys" thing?

"You know, this thing—white girls using black guys to make their white parents mad," I say. "That's kinda racist. I mean, if you think about it, right?"

Then I remind her about those stringy-haired blondes, the skanks at our all-white high school who bragged about weekend excursions to the Combat Zone where they were wicked popular because black men dug blonde girls.

"Those girls, do you remember their names? Kathy something, and Diane?"

Silence. I can hear her dragging on her cigarette at the other end of the line.

I push. "Have you ever read Eldridge Cleaver?"

Of course she hasn't.

"Hey, Linda," she says, pausing to exhale cigarette smoke, "why don't you adjust that hair across your ass?"

"Goodnight, Caroline."

—

My first day at work there, August greeted me in his apron with the New York Times. That was how it started. We were the only two people who read the paper all the way through. The boss had told him that we'd like each other—both of us big readers.

I had run away from home to the Midwest, where I had a Catholic friend in St. Paul who was like an older sister. Every day at my new job in Minneapolis, we served lunch to old people in the dining room, or brought it to them at home if they couldn't come to us. Sometimes August needed help in the kitchen, and I was nothing if not a helper. At first, we talked about books—food and books. He loved libraries as much as I did and he knew a lot about poetry, and could recite things from memory. I had never heard of John Berryman or John Wieners until he told me about them. And I had never known a writer, except for my brother Joey.

I was darker than he was, because I'd been outside all summer. He had known Irish and Italian Catholic girls like me in Pittsburgh. Had gone to Catholic school with them, until he dropped out.

The stories he told about the people he'd known—the stories he told about his own life—it was as if he were a mythological character. His first kiss. His mother. The time he spent his last dollar on the finest hat in a store window. His hours at counters in coffee shops, listening and scribbling. Him with the blues and the record player.

He told me an anecdote or two about his sexual history—to shock me, I guess, and I was shocked—but it was the stories about money and the blues that made me question all my assumptions about virtue. Spending instead of saving? Buying a hat instead of paying your debts? The point was, mores were cultural, and though I didn't want to admit it to him, he was making me question mine. In his kitchen, he looked at me as if I'd be delicious. He listened to me, too, and remembered everything I said, and challenged me in ways no one had challenged me. Especially when he was angry (or performing anger).

I showed him some poems I had written—love poems about a man I'd met when I worked at Harvard. Then he wrote poems for me on napkins, poems that were too grand for my taste. I threw them away. I didn't want to be a cliché—a naïve young woman, like my illegitimate father's poor mother, seduced and abandoned—or that other cliché, a white woman with a black man.

Anyway, he was married (to his second wife, a white woman). And he smoked, and I hated cigarettes. He made all kinds of promises I was sure he couldn't keep—he'd bring me to New York—he knew his plays were going to be on Broadway—and buy me dresses. I laughed at his blandishments.

But then he gave me his typescript for Ma Rainey. *I read it in the back seat of a car on a trip to Chicago, surrounded by my wholesome co-workers. When I got back to Minneapolis, I looked at him differently. He was what he said he was. A writer.*

One grey afternoon, after we cleaned the kitchen, after everyone else had gone home, he pulled a pint of whiskey out of a cabinet and brought me and two shot glasses and a piece of pound cake (his specialty) into the empty dining hall. There he performed parts of the play he was writing, including Troy's monologue about (dialogue with) Death.

The next day, after we cleaned the kitchen, I drove him home.

"What are you going to do now?" I asked.

"I'm gonna go rest on the couch and listen to the blues."

"I want a job like that," I said.

"Then be a writer," he growled, and he walked away, adjusting his cap and tucking his notebook up into his armpit so he could put his hands in his pockets. Winter came so early there.

I liked him best when he was gruff with me, telling me what to do when helping him in the kitchen, and criticizing me for wanting to be respectable. "Don't hate what you come from," he said. "That's like hating yourself."

It was when he told me I was beautiful that the trouble started.

He was fourteen years older than I was, and he was so relentless and intense; now I think I would just laugh it off—"Men!"—but then I felt I had no choice but to leave. I couldn't just ignore him—he was the only person worth talking to. All the others were Midwestern do-gooders. I didn't belong there.

When he saw me putting my suitcases near the door, he was angry.

"Where are you going?" he said, shocked at how quickly I was packing up.

"You're married," I said. "Leave me alone."

"But you blossomed under my attention!" he said.

This was true.

"What about your wife?" I said.

He believed in marriage, he said, "As an institooooution."

I frowned. I knew nothing about life, but I knew that when you got married, you took a vow.

—

When I got back to Boston and moved to Somerville with a high school friend, I went into an androgynous phase. For wasn't it my femininity, my vanity, that had gotten me into trouble with him? I switched to gabardine shirts that hid my curves, I wore longer skirts and chunky shoes or Keds with ankle socks.

But it turned out to be impossible to get away from him, as he had said it would be. Soon he was everywhere I was—in New Haven, where I ran into him on the street, went out for a drink with him, and finally succumbed, anti-climatically (and, on High Street, threw away one last poem on a napkin)—and in New York, on Broadway and in the papers. I never saw him again, except at a production of Fences; he beamed with delight when he saw me on the stairs. I was married by then, and surprised to see him. The play had been up for a long time and he was still attending performances? I smiled, looked down, and headed for the exit.

I worked in midtown for eight years as he got more and more famous, and I couldn't avoid the publicity when his plays were on stage in New York. The haunting was a continuing education, a vexation and a comedy, and a lesson in the stamina and determination it took to be a writer. But I avoided Broadway when I knew he was in town. I was afraid I would run into him again, be cast under his spell.

In the spring of 1995, after Isabel was finished with her colic, after I'd learned to nurse easily and anywhere, I went back to work. One spring day I brought her to Manhattan with me. On the way to my office I sat in Bryant Park and nursed her, and then she sat in my lap and babbled about the flowers printed on my skirt. Giving birth and being a mother made me feel powerful. The sun was shining. I wished one of his plays was in town, wished I could go find him in the Edison coffee shop and show him who I'd become and what I'd done. "You were right," I'd say. "I am beautiful. And look what I made! I made something beautiful!"

And then, a few years later, when I was 37, the age he was when he enchanted and confused me, I left my marriage and seduced a younger man. Exercising the powers I finally had, or could finally own up to.

—

Isabel is with Andrew for two nights. I'm trying to get off antidepressants. A racket in my brain—the synapses, squirrels rustling through dry leaves, looking for nuts, desperate because winter's coming.

I don't want to be on drugs for the rest of my life, I don't want to be numbed into submission.

I am going back East again with Isabel. The Press will pay for my ticket, since I'm making a trip to the Vineyard to see Fanny. I'll go deeper into debt to pay for Isabel's ticket and a little cottage at Humarock, just far enough away from my parents.

Andrew's presence used to put the brakes on the worst of my mother, but now that I'm man-less, I'm afraid she might hit me like she still hits my brother. Her rage ruins everything. But my father's creepiness and misogyny is what I fear most, now that I have a little girl to protect. When I see fathers hugging their daughters, I flinch before remembering that not all fathers are like our father.

Another thing I can't talk about. Too dirty. Too wrapped up in Catholicism and shame.

"It ain't so much what the music says. It's what you can't do about it."
 – Chester Himes

—

Nightmare trip to Boston. Had a few sweet days at the beach with Isabel, but at the end I had to spend one night at my parents' house with her, and now I don't know if I'll ever see them again.

The last day of vacation, the only day I was trapped with them, I checked my voicemail messages, desperate for some news about a new job, a way out of the pressure cooker at the work. There was a message from Judy Butler: she knew of a job that would be a good fit for me, and had recommended me. I got off the phone, smiling with relief, and turned to share the news with my mother.

"I think I may have a new job!"

She dismissed me with a smirk and a wave of her hand. "Oh, you—you career girl."

I wanted to hit her.

"Do you not understand, Ma? I'm a worker. I'm a single mother. I'm living paycheck to paycheck."

Those Ladies Macbeth at the office, and my other coworkers, nice middle

-class people who have manners and common sense—normal people who understand self-interest and weren't raised to be martyrs—how would the Blessed Mother deal with office politics and single motherhood?

My mother looked disgusted. "The hell with all of you. You're all sick. All of youse."

My father was sitting in his chair, watching the news, paying no attention to this fight in the doorway from kitchen to parlor. On the TV, there was a report about child abuse, something about preschoolers.

"Poor kids," my father said, because their mothers left them there and went off to work. "But they're so little, they won't even remember," he said. And then, under his breath, he said, "Jesus, nowadays you can't get away with nothin'."

—

I've held my tongue my whole life, proud to think that I was not like the rest of them. But I couldn't let that pass. And out came the unspeakable. What he did to me when I was little. What he can't remember and I can't forget.

And what they did to the other kids—if Joey were alive he'd have burned this house down by now.

But I didn't say anything about all of that. I just talked about what I remembered that night in the kitchen sink when I was four.

"Ah, you," he said, giving me the back of his hand. "You're more trouble than you're worth."

I ran up the stairs—stairs lined with my mother's slippers, orthopedic shoes, and a stack of *Reader's Digest* and Knights of Columbus magazines. I stopped and flung some magazines down the stairs in my fury. I ran up to the landing where my mother once slammed a door on my finger, breaking it. That cramped second story where seven of us slept—or never really slept. But now it was just me and Isabel up there in the boys' old bedroom with the sloping wall.

I pushed the dresser up against the door. They are dangerous and shameless, these people who shamed us. I've seen what they'd done to the others, and I know what they will do to me, now that I am a failure, alone in the world.

I trembled, looking up at the Red Sox pennant and the St. Pauli Girl poster on the wall, as I decided to stay here for the night. I would not let them put us out the way they drove my sister and her baby out, drove Richard out, drove Joey out. When I stopped shaking I put my arms around Isabel and breathed her air. I fell asleep holding her.

We got up before dawn to head for the airport. The house was quiet. My parents had fled. I had touched a nerve, or the tip of an iceberg.

I pulled Isabel close to me and she looked up and smiled. Did she know we were fleeing? I don't think so. She was just glad we were going home.

We were so early for the flight, I detoured and stopped in the North End to show Isabel the places where we used to take Nonie to buy her yeast and her grain alcohol and the flavoring for the anisette.

I showed her Paul Revere's church and the old Sicilians eating pastry in the bakeries. We stood in the doorway of a pork store and inhaled the smell of the ancient wooden floor, the spices, the salami and the Parmesan. And then we went to Logan to catch our flight. "Only the desperate go to East Boston," Wieners wrote. From here I could almost see the tenement where my mother was born.

I looked down as we swooped over the South Shore. I was leaving the 18th, 19th, and 20th centuries for good.

A flight attendant, tall and blond, brought a warm (business-class) cookie for Isabel. And though it was not yet noon, he brought a glass of wine for me—the good stuff, the red they serve in first class, in a real glass, for free. "It's too early," I said. But I guess he could see I was having a bad day. "It's cocktail hour somewhere, dear." He was so sweet. I could easily imagine what he looked like in his fourth-grade school photo—hair parted carefully and greased back—a few missing teeth.

I gave Isabel a pad of paper and a pen. She asked me how to spell "beauty" and "joy." I wrote them down for her. Then she proceeded to write "the beauty of the joy" on every page of the pad.

Getting off the plane in San Francisco, I breathed in the smell of fog and eucalyptus. What was I coming home to? Difficulties. But better difficulties than the ones I'd left behind.

—

September 11th. In the pharmacy, collective sadness, silence, except for an autistic boy who's waiting with his grandfather for a prescription. The boy is screaming and crying, the old man is holding him tightly and tenderly. No one looks right at him. Nor does anyone move away from him.

Isabel's poems:

Mom

*This living
creature walks
around The
house not
knowing what
to do.*

Isabel

*This wonderful
creature walks
around the house
Throwing Back her
Pearls*

—

Chaperoning a school field trip. Mary Ann went on and on about being a full-time homemaker with an au pair, a cleaning lady, a dog walker and a body worker. "With two kids and a husband, the scheduling is impossible!"

I said, "That sounds like a lot to manage."

On the bus with a book about Christianity on her lap, she told me about Islam: "It's such a violent religion!" She explained that Christianity is gentle, and that's why America is a beacon of light.

More than half the kids on this bus are the descendants of people enslaved by Christians.

I told her I had to check on the kids and moved to the back of the bus.

—

Dinner here last night with Steve, Tina, Elizabeth, and kids. Broiled salmon, roasted potatoes (red, purple, and yellow), roasted peppers, green beans with sesame seeds, green tomatoes with new onions from the farmer's market. Steve asked to see my Strayhorn collages but Claudia bought them all after her book party at the Kitchen. So I showed them old collages, the ones I made in my office across from Grand Central. Cheap postcards doctored with Wite-Out and black Sharpies. The Wite-Out on the Hart Crane series is cracked now, and you can see my fingerprints.

Crane, at Melville's tomb: "Monody shall not wake the mariner."

—

I'm pierced with envy of friends who can be daughter, wife, and mother all at once. I've never had that luxury; never will.

—

Six is a nice age. Isabel spent an hour of "private time" in my room. She calls it "our room"; she has never spent a night or even an hour in her own bed in my apartment. And her room isn't really a room—it has no doors—we walk through it when we go from the hallway to the kitchen. I could hear her leaping and dancing on the bed. She was watching herself in the mirror and asked me not to look at her while she played. When she was finished, she called out. I went in and found a sort of installation—strings and ribbons and thread and tape crisscrossing the room, and the Oxford English Dictionary and magnifying glass wrapped in a pink feather boa.

———

Helping her to spell words as she writes one of her own books: "Mama, how do you spell 'world'?"

"W-O-R-"

"Yes?" she says. "Yes?"

Like the suspense is unbearable.

———

Two days before Christmas. Andrew took Isabel shopping. In the morning, I cleaned her room and found yet one more Barbie accessory, a shoe, from that 100-piece set that Park gave her for Christmas when he was wooing me. I thought I'd gotten rid of everything.

In the afternoon, I ran into Park in Temescal. We hugged awkwardly. His whiskers scraped my cheek, and I remembered the rash they left on the inside of my thigh the first time we made love—the first time I'd made love with someone other than my husband of fourteen years. How I cherished that rash.

I asked him about the holidays, and work, and I asked him if he was seeing anyone.

"Kind of," he said, and I felt a pang.

I reminded him of his promise to invite me to his wedding someday. And I wished him a merry Christmas.

On my hand I'd written the word "MILK" with a black Sharpie. A reminder to go to the market. At the store I picked up toilet paper, overpriced Tampax, and milk, and I asked the butcher if they carried sliced turkey. "No," he said grimly, shaking his head, "though we did fool around with cold cuts for a while." As if he were remembering a fling with a hussy who nearly ruined his marriage.

Feminine

Friends who do not fail us
Mary in our hour of
despair. Take not
away from me the small fires
I burn in the memory of love.

John Wieners, "A Poem for Cocksuckers"

The maiden language all over.

Zora Neale Hurston

My Mary

Does the rain have a mother?
Who made the drops of dew?
Out of whose womb came the ice?
She is hardened against her young ones
As though they were not hers.
The face of the deep is frozen.

My Mystic

For FQH

My mystic is not old enough to be my mother.

She yells "No!" when she laughs at my jokes.

She can't keep anything down and doesn't drink, except for whiskey, wine, and water.

My mystic is her father's daughter.

My mystic has her own monk, a hermit who had his own monk.

Out on a boat on the Atlantic with a friend, tossed around, my mystic screams with laughter when they don't drown.

My mystic has an early edition of Proust in a closet with her sheets and towels.

Any house sitter could steal it, but no one does.

My mystic picks at her croissant in the dark, Swann's Way in her lap.

My mystic wants to know all about my men, so I tell her and she groans, and then we talk about the new Pope. She thinks he has a humble face.

From her apartment we can see an orange neon sign across the Cambridge green. At dusk it tints the dirty snow.

My mystic used to run in and out of that hotel lobby with her best friend, stealing candy.

Now children crawl all over my mystic. In the pockets of her vest (the color of their red toboggan) they find hard candy.

My mystic is a sister. Is lilacs. Is toast.

My mystic has already bought her plot.

My mystic is both the crone and the infant in the fairy tale.

My mystic is a fairy. She flies everywhere but leaves no carbon footprint.

My mystic has a device. Children text my mystic from L. A., Dubai,
    Oxford, Paris.

My mystic might have been named Affliction or Delight if born at sea
    in 1620.

Or, two centuries later, out of Cobh and mad in steerage: perhaps
    Theresa.

My mystic has lips the color of a rose named for the Cathars,
    who had but one sacrament: consolation.

Small Square

A blue peninsula, three sides and an edge,
the answer to triangulation, my issue—
frame and boundary versus
unholy trinity. This texture takes paint
well, this size is my size. One thousand
little things add up.

•

Saw yesterday at 5:15 PM:
a billowing cloud
moving across the suddenly
blue sky. A perfect
window, a SQUARE—
a word that should have
just four letters—opened up
in the body of the cloud,
a kind of stanza in air.

•

I didn't gauge the distance from
the lip of the glass
to my own lip
and died laughing at what
fell in my lap.
The possibility of the personal
impersonal, the needle in my drink—
I can use it to scratch the surface.

•

The drone of radio rosaries
as I gouged a missalette—
Today I cut to ribbons
a list of "known abusers."
One of those priests used to sit at our table
laughing with my mother,
eating cake. His thick cloud of hair
lit up the room. At his wake
my mother raved about it.

•

Pieces of men all over my desk,
two skies, you but never me,
the history of photography,
Wite-Out and varnish.
I like the precision of scissors.
Where is my pot of glue?
Where is my pen?
I should do something with this.
I dip my brush into my drink.

•

You with your lips in ruins,
saturated—I don't do much with purple
so your windmill of a mind
may not show up this time.
The etymology of your soul is
your business.

•

When I was small but no longer young
I decided, building moats and dikes,
to use a neutral color, pale as a desert boot.
Even then I was famous for my values.
Now I mix glitter into cement.
You wouldn't know me.

•

Remember my limited palette,
cracked panels and angels
entering frames like explanations.
Forgive my blue note, my halo, my
shitty materials.
Forgive me, and look at me
while I am talking to you,
or at least picture my face.

Begin in Blue

The blue of her robe . . . reads above all as a flat silhouetted shape—a deep infinite midnight blue, large enough to lose ourselves in . . . this very dark blue creates unparalleled effects . . . almost of hypnotic trance; it is as though we are being invited to worship not so much the Madonna as the Blue.

Timothy Hyman, *Sienese Painting*

I'm reading John Wieners' chapbook, *Pressed Wafer*, at one of the giant tables upstairs in the archives where I work, when a visiting scholar asks for help with research. And that's how I learn that, in 1882, landscape architects at the University of California designed a eucalyptus grove for the Berkeley campus (a grove through which I walk once a week). Tasmanian blue gum trees were planted as a windbreak for the cinder running track. They grew and grew, non-natives making themselves at home. To one who'd never seen a eucalyptus tree, the grove must have smelled like cough drops.

Wieners was a Boston boy. Later, in San Francisco, he wore blue eye shadow and sold heroin packed in matchboxes the size of a palette of eye shadow—false eyelashes, glued one above the other on his forehead—cockeyed Caucasian—

Eyelids the color and shape of the leaves of the blue eucalyptus near the track where the beautiful athlete, also a Joseph, also a John, breathing hard after a sprint, does not look up at the plane from Boston passing over the track—

Boys in California know nothing of priests in long skirts shoveling snow, winters invented by Emily Dickinson—

The Blacks and the blues,
the grove as artifice—

In Berkeley, Robert Creeley recorded a version of "A Poem for Painters":

"With want of it"—
"despair is on my face"—
"showered by the scent of the finish line"—

The golden boys protected by tall trees—
blue blood—blue eucalyptus—blue-lined paper—
"beginning with violet. I begin in blue"—
"My middle name is Joseph"—

•

Sanskrit "vaka"
"wat" (temple)
"grove" (copse, thicket)—
A coppice—spinney—brake—for the broken—

A grove: a stand of trees with little or no undergrowth—So here's the
floor, all clear and still, a thicket—"cold hell"—

Grave Love Leaves

Torn tickets in the eucalyptus leaves, pants in the trees—

Who walks through the grove in winter rain? Pants decomposing in the
decomposing leaves— pants, and a dog—

This was after the picturesque era, before Free Speech— "Books in the
running brooks," books in the trees—

•

Strawberry Creek roars with the snowmelt coming down from Truckee.
The train back to Boston leaves at 3:00.

Across the "enormous" country—passing a car filled with Beats, ascend-
ing, going where Beats don't go—

Climbing into the mountains he leans out the window, his ears pasted back like a dog's—like a dog, submissively free— submission is different when there's no force.

In the Rockies they close the windows now because so many travelers have been decapitated leaning out to see the trees—but the windows were open then, so he looked—looked—looked—

A Parakeet

Titus, her father, had made a voyage to the Indies, and brought back with him a green parrowkeet, the first of its kind to be seen in Dorset.

Sylvia Townsend Warner, *Lolly Willowes*

The children throw things at you.
You have nowhere to go.
You're like something to be melted down
And stuck with a wick while talking.

When it's gloomy outside they sit in front of you
As if you were a fire.
It's gloomy inside, too.

You don't mean to be entertaining,
Gesticulating with one nervous but adamant claw,
Waving the alternate cut wing for emphasis—

Articulate as the sleeve of a revivalist's robe
(That is, inarticulate)
As she measures a storefront she once owned
or plans to own,
"God willing."
For they have taught you to say
"God willing."

Of course there is no reason for birds to talk
Or to be as colorful as lollipops.
Perhaps like women they "know they are dynamite,
And long for the concussion
That may justify them."

Feminine

Last night when I said I was king
he pulled me closer.

Words Looking for a Street

And most of all when you have forgotten Sunday.

Gwendolyn Brooks

"What is the answer to this ragged eating?" my brother wrote long ago, two years before he died. A question that still nags. What should I do? For now, I'll be with you. My feet in your lap, we drink drink after drink at a place in the Castro, the first gay bar with windows. From the mezzanine I smell cookies baking, sweetness fluming from a vent. Downstairs three grey men, survivors of the plague, are talking about a jerk. A loner reads Augustine next to us. He doesn't seem to notice us canoodling.

But as he leaves he stops to say, "You two are sweet together." You beam in that way that makes me nervous, and I realize he's been eavesdropping all the while. He's heard us talk about your trial, your celebrity witnesses, my memories of the projects and the lady who gave us her back issues of *Jet*. Heard us discuss Baraka and famous playwrights we have known. Heard me explain my Sinatra theory. Heard you tell me about Ayler's ghosts and mothers and Bob Kaufman's vow of silence.

Did he hear you say that you want to go shopping for panties with me? He must have heard me bark with laughter: "Who, me?"

Yes, we are sweet.

How did we survive when others were convicted, others died? And why are we here?

Because you were acquitted. Because I didn't kill myself. Because the Thai place doesn't open until five.

In My Girlish Days

It took the 8-year-old female [shark] 21 hours to eat the 5-year-old male inside a tank at the aquarium. According to video of the consumption, the female shark started with the male's head and slowly went about consuming the rest of his body. This act of shark cannibalism likely was the result of the sharks bumping into one another. "Sharks have their own territories," an aquarium official told Reuters. "Sometimes, when they bump into each other, they bite out of astonishment."

Twenty-one hours?
I would have made a meal of him
in the time it takes to listen
to every song on Sinatra's
In the Wee Small Hours
("the greatest break-up album of all time")

but then I'd spend the rest of my life
feeling terrible about it—
"I'm sorry, dear—
you astonished me,
so I ate you."

I eat men like air
or something.

Foundress of Nothing: Journals

Trying to run away from that home of mine
I didn't know no better
Oh boys
In my girlish days

Memphis Minnie

2002

La Mala Femmina

New Year's Day

Divorce came through yesterday, the last day of the worst year after a lifetime of some pretty awful years. I tried to postpone it—my life is falling apart, I have no money for a lawyer—but Andrew insisted he had to get it done right now—maybe for tax purposes?

I said he should give me something for all the things I'd paid for over the years—his Yale loans, rent on his studio, paints and the car, his parking tickets—and the cost of moving into our new apartment after he broke our lease and moved in with his parents. He said that a judge might force ME to give him alimony, since I have a job and he's an artist. When he told me that his lawyer said they could go after my pension, I gave up.

He's off to his parents' vacation home for the weekend. I remember going up there when Isabel was a baby, when I knew I had to do the unthinkable and leave the marriage. I remember standing in that gorgeous house, thinking, "I'll have to give all of this up. I will give this up."

He just bought himself a two-thousand-dollar bike.

And I am *la mala femmina*. The bad woman. Cast out—

His mother was divorced, his grandmother was divorced, his uncle was divorced. I never knew anyone who was divorced when I was growing up. Divorce was forbidden. And too expensive for people like us.

I can hardly breathe. But I still have to raise Isabel with him. And I will do it right, and he will, too. And she'll have something I didn't have—a mother and a father. A real family.

———

New job. Lonely editorial work. But now I don't have to travel and I work in a research library. Databases galore, online censuses, maps, newspapers. I search the ruins of maiden names, and the stigma of my father's illegitimacy looms again. Is it pathetic to try to make meaning of all this chaos and shame? I feel like I'm a dog pawing at a grave. But I have this document—the social worker's report about my grandmother's case— when she was indigent, unmarried, with child—my father—in 1932 and '33. I pore over it, I search for birth and death certificates and graves. Lost women and children. Ghosts beckon in the ether.

Googling, I learn that the Black Valley, where my father's mother grew up, was the last place in Ireland to get electricity—in 1978!

I go down to the stacks and borrow every book I can find about Kerry in the early twentieth century, and the Civil War there, and madness and women and illegitimacy in Ireland.

—

"A divorce is like a death, but instead of that inevitable end, the person that we have loved stands there as a living reproach of deep failure." – *John McGahern*

The Church shamed him, as it shamed so many Irish writers, and sent him into exile for telling the truth, but he never left the Church.

—

Every day I read "Portraits of Grief" in the *NYT*—palm-sized obituaries of people who died on the planes or in and around the buildings on September 11th. Today, with a gasp, I recognized a face—that flight attendant who was so kind to us when we flew out of Boston the morning after that terrible fight. He was flying to LA on the eleventh, trying to pick up extra shifts so he could take a long vacation.

—

Margaret told me that Emma kept telling her "Isabel's mom is devoted." It took a while for Margaret to realize that she meant "divorced." Emma doesn't know anyone else whose parents are divorced.

—

"What is death?"

The day they ask. Or the day you have to tell them—

I was looking at a picture album with her on the couch, showing her the one of Nonie with Pa, fresh off the boat, posed in finery. He sits, the patriarch, the bully, and she stands behind him, a look of unspeakable pain on her face. The old man of 35 went back to Sicily to get himself a bride, a servant for his tyrannical, poor, illiterate parents in their tenement in East Boston.

I turn the page to the pictures of us kids. I say each of our names. "Linda, Caroline, Richard, Joey, Michael." I notice for the first time that Joey's standing next to me in each of the pictures.

"The little kids," she says. "And you were the big one."

———

Today I drove around and around, focused intently on trying to find a place to park on Lakeshore.

"Mama," she said from her car seat, watching my face in the rearview mirror, "are you sad because you're thinking about your brother who died?"

"No, honey," I said, astonished. "I'm just worried because I can't find a parking spot."

———

Re-reading *Long Day's Journey into Night*. The bitterness starts on page 42, with Mary, of course. "Bitterly resentful"—"Bitterly"—"Bitterly"—"Her bitterness receding." Tyrone: "A tired, bitterly sad old man." Jamie: "Bitterly." I count thirty-three instances of bitterness in the stage directions in this play about an Irish American family. The characters also do things angrily, violently, pleadingly, hopelessly, pitifully, philosophically, stupidly, pathetically, resentfully, tenderly, miserably, contemptuously, provocatively, and, of course, sentimentally.

Don't be bitter, Linda.

———

My cassette tape-to-tape player died, and I'm so sad—it's like the death of a pet—the end of an era. I got so many cassettes at that shitty little record shop on Fulton St. in Brooklyn—run by Koreans for a largely black clientele—me like a ghost in those crowds—walking hours and hours in Brooklyn while Andrew was in Greenpoint in the studio—Public Enemy, Run DMC, Son House, Edwin Hawkins and Tramaine, D Train, Memphis Minnie, Inez Andrews, Sister Lyn Collins the Female Preacher, and Tower of Power. The streets of Brooklyn were my Harvard and my Yale, and that was my sacred music.

—

I go to the doctor, she tells me there's a new class of antidepressant, one that has no sexual side effects. She gives me a sample and I look at the small print. Manufactured in the country of sexually repressed depressives, the Republic of Ireland. Who knew? I tell the doctor that my father's mother was from Ireland—that her mother died young of "melancholy" and "worry" in the lunatic asylum there. But I'm mumbling and the doctor doesn't hear me. Anyway, it's not like this is a therapy session.

"OK, I'll try it."

I who would not even take Advil for my hideous PMS, who went through labor with no pain meds, who believed in suffering, will do whatever it takes to be a good mother, to survive.

—

Richard says Ma and Dad are telling everyone in Boston that I'm crazy, I'm insane, and a liar.

But still I try to keep them connected to their granddaughter at a safe distance. And I pray for them. And for myself.

The box of Christmas gifts for Isabel, things coming out of the wrapping paper, pages from the *Boston Globe*—a crumpled picture of Osama Bin Laden yielding a doll, a flower bulb, a tin of pizzelle. We used to throw pizzelle in the air to make the dog jump in the kitchen. Nonie cried at the waste. "*Bedda matri mia!*"

She didn't say "*Mamma mia*" like Italians in the movies. Why? It occurs to me to look it up. "*Bedda matri mia*" is dialect—an echo of Arabs in Sicily—the Internet explains.

The town my mother's mother came from, I learned in a museum catalogue, was a Jewish settlement until Jews were expelled in the 1400s.

I help Isabel write a thank-you note, mail it, drop her off with Andrew, and go to Kingman's. A Manhattan, a glass of wine. Sadness.

—

I am re-reading *Raisin in the Sun*, noticing Ruth's and Beneatha's stage directions. There are poems in them:

(Sadly)

(Turning to him) (Almost automatically)
(Indifferently)

(Mocking) (Mimicking) (Simply
and with flavor)

(Bitterly) (With a frown) (Softly)
(Drily, but to hurt)

(She rises) (She gets money) (Tenderly)
(Angrily)

(Exasperated) (Laughing) (Sincerely
but self-righteously)

(Keeps her head down, ironing) (They laugh)
(For devilment)

(Glad to add kindling almost gently,
with profound understanding)

2003

"There wouldn't be an 'I.'"

Picked Isabel up at JCC. She was disappointed she was not chosen as mensch of the week. But then Lily came out and told her she was being cast as the princess in the family Shabbat play and she was happy. We drove to Green Gulch. She was surprised to find herself right at home. "So far, Mom, I love this."

I told her she could go for a walk with the other little girl staying in the guesthouse. "'OK," she said, "or I'll just go for a walk with my own subconscious."

In the garden she performed for me: "Mom, look, I'm making up my own national dance." Swallows flew under the eaves of the zendo. Our room has walls made out of plaster and straw, a little like a swallow's nest. We visited all the shrines and she asked me, "Mom, do Zens believe in God?"

———

Emerson: "We learn geology the day after the earthquake."

We learn marriage in the years after the divorce.

———

Mica schist, the geological foundation of the skyscrapers of New York—

A week after the closing ceremonies at Ground Zero they found twelve bodies in a nearby building. So much for closure.

"Moloch, moloch, moloch . . ." Someone is reading (very quietly and unnervingly) Allen Ginsberg's poem on TV.

———

The hyphen in my holy-ness. My un-assimilation—

Isabel and I had a social day with Emma and then with our many guests. When we'd sent everyone home, she took my face in her hands and said one word: "Love."

—

Palm Sunday

Waking slowly from a dream yesterday as if pressed into the bed by force, as if I'd been dropped from a great height, the 110th story of my dreams and nightmares

Andrew is in Monterey riding his bike. His second or is it his third childhood? I'm paying for this one, too. Feeling low and lost and old; Isabel should not be stuck with such a mother. But then it always turns out to be fine. We make a world. We ate lunch at 15ᵗʰ and Webster, then walked to the children's room at the OPL. Took our books to the lawn at the lake, wished we could row back across the water to our apartment, which we could almost see from there. I finished O'Faolain's *Are You Somebody* and she read her book about monsters. She asked me to read bits aloud and so I learned for the first time about yetis.

Andrew reads *Harry Potter* to her when she's over there. I can't read aloud more than a few sentences without falling back into my Boston accent. I don't mind, but my voice is too weak for long books like Rowling's.

On the way home, from the back seat, Isabel breaks our silence: "Mom, what does 'ignorance' mean?"

I'm hit again and again with the force of what it really means to be a little girl—in my mind I never was one. The oldest child. Older than my parents, really. They were the youngest in their big families.

Isabel, pondering the riddle of existence: "If I didn't exist, I'd feel so bad about not existing. But there wouldn't be an 'I' to have the feeling."

—

I remember Ma and then Dad slapping books out of my hands, telling me there was no escape, I couldn't hide. Maybe that's mostly what books were for me—a way to hide, a way to shield my face and eyes.

Now I break up with men so I'll have more time to read.

—

For Isabel, an only child, normal bickering between siblings seems terrifying. I told her it was normal for brothers and sisters to fight; everything will be OK, at least for her friends who have judicious, grown-up parents. My family was more like the Sopranos or a Joe Orton farce.

I walked down to the lake with Isabel and Emma on Sunday. They ran ahead and Isabel shouted back to me, with pure exuberance; "Mama, is it OK if I pretend to be mad at Emma so people will think we're sisters?"

I wrote something about my brothers last week and showed it to Toni. We met to talk about it today. "The narrator mentions the sister," she said. "Is the sister an important character?"

"Oh yes. Much too important to write about."

—

I was the good girl, she was bad. I was smart, she learned to play dumb. We were positioned in the family to be complete opposites, yet were usually addressed as "You girls," as if it were too much trouble to see us or to say our names.

Ma, driving home from the garage where she got the kind of attention from mechanics that she could not get from my father, singing coyly to herself: "I love coffee, I love tea, I love the boys and the boys love me."

The boys love us.

—

So I went online, because my married friends say that's what I should do, and I found someone, Bob, a PG&E dispatcher (he used to be a lineman) who was recruited not long ago from the Midwest. He works twelve-hour shifts, which is good for me because I would only have to see him every so often. He was affectionate and earthy and a great kisser, and he fixed my broken rocking chair and my kitchen faucet and the light over the stove. And he was generous. One night when I had planned to watch a video with Isabel, our VCR broke and he surprised us by driving through the rain on his motorcycle with a new VCR strapped to the back of the bike. (Still I didn't let him stay over while Isabel was with me; I'll never let anyone do that.)

But before long I noticed that some things didn't add up. He'd actually been divorced not twice, as he had told me, but three times, and he had cheated on the first two wives, and, though he had vowed to change (he'd found the Lord, he said), I didn't believe him. He has a bunch of kids from two wives and it turns out he likes Bush. How someone who could like Bush could like me, I do not know, but he insisted it wasn't a problem (for him).

His oldest daughter and his two youngest kids came to visit on a long-planned trip from the Midwest. We had a great time with them and they seemed to love me (though he later told me that Tiffany had said to him, "Linda is such a nice traditional person, so how can she like Clinton and abortion?"). The next night we all piled into my car after pizza near Bob's condo. Suddenly Tiffany's mood changed. Apparently she'd seen from the car one of the few black men in this famously white suburb, Walnut Creek. He was walking down the street near her father's gated community.

"Is this a bad area?" she asked. Even in the dark I could see the terror on her face. Bob had seen the guy too. It was like they had some kind of color radar. Bob told Tiffany it wasn't dangerous here, but where I lived was a jungle; then he promised he would protect her and me with his life if any of them attacked us.

The next time I was alone with Bob and he touched me, I berated him with such contempt that he fell into his childhood stutter. I kind of hated myself for treating him that way, for reducing the man to a boy (something I am too good at doing). He's been very loving to me, and I need love. But when he started crying and told me he wanted to build us a house in Walnut Creek and get us out of Oakland, I told him it was over.

—

In New York again, visiting Eve and Arthur and Colette and Stanley, and walking, walking, walking. On the street on the way down to the WTC, the smell of cooking meat, and on the curb, a box of chicken feet on ice.

At the Met: Corpus from a Cross without the cross, so Christ crucified appears to float freely in the case. Florentine and Sienese paintings, my favorites: heads thrown back so they look like platters on necks—lamentation, adoration, pleading—

The balconies, the plaster of the buildings, the sky—pink—

The invention of perspective—when did that happen?

I walked past Sotheby's. When Andrew was an art handler he got tickets to an auction of contemporary art. Everyone was so well groomed, thin, elegantly dressed—that class of people I'd first seen at the Beaux Arts Ball at Yale. At the auction, I was wearing five-dollar black pants and a black rayon sweater and chunky shoes. I leaned against a light fixture on the wall until a guard approached and I realized it was a Dan Flavin sculpture.

Andrew always wished I would dress better. On our second date, he and his friends cut my hair and spiked it with gel. Later they took me to the vintage store and picked out a tweed coat for me. At the Goodwill in Williamsburg Andrew would always notice the real finds—expensive things, imported fabric. But I couldn't see it. To me, all black clothes looked the same.

—

I went to Arthur's and Grace's place for Shabbat. Grace, a WASP, lit the candles and said the blessing about Ephraim and Manasseh for Eli and Nathan. No brother against brother in that house. I found it very moving.

The next day I had lunch with Stanley in Queens and told him about

Shabbat. "Grace is Protestant but she's the best Jewish mother ever," I said, marveling.

He shrugged his shoulders and said, "Sometimes that happens."

—

Back in Oakland . . .

He's a painter's painter
He's a cyclist's cyclist
And I'm alone

—

"Her first dream was dead so she became a woman." – Zora Neale Hurston

Behind the counter at the Quikmart, pints of Wild Turkey for guys who sleep on sidewalks. Big red sticker: "New unbreakable bottle!"

—

Bel is with Andrew today. Reading on my blanket, I fall sleep in the rose garden near a bed of American Beauty roses. Across the path, they are setting up for a ceremony. A wedding harpist shows up and flirts with a kitty in the grass. "Ooh, you're so fat, who feeds you?" This place is like something out of Disney today, but someone was attacked at the top of the garden last week.

"Do you speak Farsi?" asks an older wedding guest who's lost.

"No," I say, accustomed to being mistaken for Iranian (or Greek or Lebanese or whatever) because of my dark hair and eyes and eyebrows.

I tell her that I got the darkness from both sides of the family.

"You're Irish and Sicilian, what a combination! You like to drink, you have a bad temper?"

Yes and yes. But I had a fuse so long that I didn't explode until I was 37.

The harpist's name is Olga. She comes from Odessa. The police interrupt us to tell us she must move her harp.

"Are you married?" Olga asks as she lugs the thing. When I say no, she's puzzled. I get this a lot. I still don't really know how not to be married.

———

Watching *Stuart Little* with Isabel. In the credits there's a glorious shot of the New York skyline, the Twin Towers. The social worker visits the Littles to tell them that Stuart's real parents—mice—were killed in a terrible accident long ago—crushed by cans of cream of mushroom soup in a grocery store. "They had to identify them by their dental records."

———

The other day I had to stop for a funeral cortege near the cemetery that Olmsted designed. I used to see such processions all the time when I lived in New England and New York, but here they're rare.

I was listening to Mahalia Jackson's "If You See My Savior" on a CD that Young gave me when we were close and spent so much time together. A cop holding one of those old-fashioned funeral signs directed the traffic with much self-importance, unaware that the sign was upside down.

———

Dinner with Steve and Tina. Steve gets a call and I hear him talking about an alcoholic relation who is being released from the hospital because he's better. "But how much better can he be," asks Steve, "if gangrene has set in?"

———

Isabel has composed a score with notes and sounds

> *la la la la bing dingeling*
> *la la la la bing dingeling*
> *Pine forest*
> *Chorus: [spelled "chores"]: Bay leaves*
> *Chorus: Blue violet bing ding-ding*

———

Drink at Kingman's with Allen, a guy I met online. He's Jewish from New York, and lives down near the fire demo site. Pretty off-the-grid (no job). Makes old-fashioned musical instruments, and he dumpster dives. Two years ago, he had a kid with a woman he barely knows.

I hear a lot of this sort of thing on dates. Apparently, there are quite a few 35- to 40-year-old single women who are trying to get pregnant with any-old-who before it's too late.

I'm lucky that it was easy to get pregnant at what turned out to be the end of a long marriage to someone I loved so much. Someone who knew Nonie, knew Joey. Knew the house I grew up in. Knew me. No way I could handle hustling to get pregnant with a stranger I met online.

I asked Allen lots of questions, undeterred by his attempts at flirtation.

He tried to keep up, answering everything, then gulped his beer and said, "You know, you're an unusual combination—half Gina Lollobrigida, half Karl Malden in *The Streets of San Francisco.*"

I covered my face and burst out laughing. (Is my nose really as big as Karl Malden's?) What a brilliant observation!

But it didn't make me want to kiss him.

—

Nightmare about a bad date, fending him off while trying to explain in detail the story behind every striation of the stretch marks on the lower left side of my belly.

—

After the reading at 21 Grand I went home and cooked tortellini for Isabel. We sat talking at the table. She chewed thoughtfully.

"Isn't it funny," she said, "that when you're thinking and talking, one thing makes you think of another thing and then another thing?"

"Yes. There's a name for that—stream of consciousness."

"Oh," she says. "I have that a lot."

———

Last month I went to a conference about words and music and met a composer who wants to collaborate on a project about prisoners with children. She got me an invitation to visit San Quentin. But I didn't pass the security clearance. When I told my host, she said, "That happens to all the best people. Just try again."

So I did, and I passed. And I went.

Glorious fall day. Sparkling views of the Pacific and San Francisco. Sad gatehouse stocked with dozens of stripped-down, dingy grey baby strollers. Sign inside the prison reminding visitors that officials do not negotiate with prisoners for hostages. Enter at your own risk.

The prison historian gives me a tour. We pass hundreds of men, most of them black. The head of the correctional officer's union comes up to say hello. He points out that PhDs come into the prison to teach the inmates how to read. "Why don't they teach us?" he says, noting that lots of the guards hardly know how to read.

I'm shown the part of the prison that serves as sweat lodge, Christian church, synagogue, mosque, whatever is needed; all inmates are guaranteed a place to worship as they please. I see the reception area, the men in orange suits, the glorious garden the inmates cultivate.

"So pretty!"

"Isn't it?" says the guard. "But look around—anything you don't see in this garden?"

"No—looks like they've got every kind of flower."

"But there's something missing—something you'd usually see in the fall in a garden."

I don't know what to say.

"Pumpkins," he says. "They can't grow pumpkins. And you know why?

Because there's a law on the books that says prisoners can't grow anything they can eat. Cause Sysco has all the contracts for all the food coming into the facilities."

I picture those enormous trucks. That frozen food. Pallets of cans. Lobbyists, dollar signs.

I remember the recipe for Pruno—liquor you can make in the toilet in your cell, using whatever you might have on hand. Can you make it out of flower petals? Marigolds, sunflowers, weeds?

Then the guy brings me to look at the cages where inmates on death row exercise. Like dog runs.

2004

The Innocency

In New York, staying with Colette on William Street. Tourists swarming everywhere, asking how to get to 9/11.

An ad for a luggage store in SOHO: "We're not Stalinists or bulimics but we must purge."

An ad for cufflinks on a subway train: "Finally: closure."

Twice on this trip strangers asked me, "Where are you from?" and when I said, "Boston," they said, "No, really, where are you from?" Meaning, which foreign country. Because a face like mine doesn't look plain American. "Are you Lebanese, Persian, Italian, Greek?" Occasionally someone even guesses that there's Irish in me. It is not a bad way to make new friends.

—

Home again. Edith Wharton and Henry James spent an afternoon together at her estate in the Berkshires and one of them wrote, "Summer afternoon: the most beautiful words in the English language." Living in Oakland I think the most beautiful words might be "Butterscotch Cadillac."

—

"Get Up Offa That Thing" plays at the end of the movie *Harriet the Spy*. I tell Isabel that James Brown was the Godfather of Soul and she says, "Who was the father?"

We don't know. Maybe Soul, like my own father, was the child of a musician passing through town. An illegitimate child.

I wonder about the words for "bastard" in various cultures—the denotations and connotations.

—

While I read a little book about the Renaissance, Isabel decides she wants to cook something. She looks into Julia Child's *The Way to Cook* and decides on crepes. I force myself to sit on the couch and not help her. She puts her ingredients on the counter and then, instead of pulling them toward her, she goes around the counter to each ingredient and adds it to her mix.

At the stove she becomes so confident that she puts her hand on her hip as she flips the crepes. I try not to laugh.

She tells me that she and her friend Sophie think that it might be fun to work at NASA, not as astronauts but as something else. She flips a crepe and it lands on the floor.

I ask, "What other kinds of jobs are there at NASA?"

She turns down the flame and comes to show me a list of new vocabulary words in her *National Geographic Kids* magazine.

"Well, actually, I've found a kind of job that sounds good for me and Sophie: 'A sinecure: a position for which little or no work is expected but for which an income is received.' Can you do that at NASA?"

—

Isabel wrote a poem after Lyn's poetry reading last night:

A pink Irony
Fills the Alphabet

Tame Wild Rice
Three word irony

—

Who was the first person in history to ever put a cut flower in a vase? The first person to make a vase? The first person to throw a drink in someone's face?

"U.S. Troops Have Damaged Babylon." And searchers keep looking for bodies in Indonesia. None will admit the work bothers them. "I am not afraid of it, of ghosts or something. If a ghost comes to haunt me, I will just ask where his body is so I can pick him up."

—

Two more poems from Isabel—she used a spell from her Book of Spells to make these:

> *In a hope that*
> *the relatively easy*
> *Exhaustion*
> *It's the daily buzz*
> *romantic*
> *Jill Scott*
> *sacrifice the things*

and

> *southeast asia*
> *you've changed*

—

In New York again. I can't afford these trips but I need them. Downstairs from Eve's, in the window of the pet store, puppies prancing on piles of cut paper. People stop to look. One man is overwhelmed and shouts at the passers-by, "Oh, would you look at the innocency!" Like something my mother would say.

I had a nightmare before the trip, the usual recurring suitcase-packing dream—surrounded by piles of stuff, I'm about to miss the plane, can't find Isabel, all that. Sometimes I call out for help. "Michael! Caroline! Richard!" But no one answers, no one can hear me.

This time my own voice woke me up. Woke Isabel, too. She said, "It's OK, I'm here," and fell back to sleep.

—

Home. In the woods with Isabel today, we found a place fit for fairies. Everything was damp and green. In a picnic table a peace sign was carved and the moss was filling in the crevices. I said, "I like the way the moss is growing in the grooves." Isabel said, "I like it too. You can tell from the moss how long people have wanted peace."

—

Last week on the plane Isabel and I were seated apart. I asked the man to my left if he would change seats. He said, "I prefer the aisle." The woman on my right said she would move. A few hours later I looked at the book in the guy's lap just in time to read the page in his thriller where the hero enters a gorgeous woman and climaxes immediately.

—

Richard calls, tells me he pulled his own tooth yesterday. He took nothing to numb it. He doesn't drink any more.

I feel bad for him. He got it worst.

I tell him I'll send some coconut cake. It's moist so it will keep in the mail, and he can eat it while he heals. I make it with stout but the alcohol burns off so it's harmless.

I sniffle and he says, "What's the matter?"

"Nothing," I say.

Is he worried about me? I've never known him to worry about me. I hesitate. I tell him I miss Isabel when she's with Andrew. I feel like a failure. I get no respect at work. Lonely. Broke. No family. My car is a shit heap. My apartment's tiny. Isabel should have her own room with a door, but I can't afford another place.

He says, "You got a daughter, a job, a place to live, and a car. You're not a failure."

—

Before Poppy Fabric opens in the morning there are seamstresses waiting at the door. At the hardware store men wait in the parking lot. People line up in front of the methadone clinic at 8:50. There's a crowd on the library steps before it opens at noon.

I changed my phone number, afraid of predators after a date with yet another creep I met online. But now I have the number of a woman who also wanted to avoid calls. I get desperate calls from a guy at the Martinez Correctional Facility who's looking for someone named Cheree. Finally I accepted the charges because I felt I should let the guy know that Cheree's not at this number anymore. He was crushed and I was sorry. If I had never been desperate myself, I wouldn't have accepted the charges.

It didn't even occur to me to worry that he'd call again. And he hasn't.

—

At Julie's and Tim's for Mother's Day. We told the kids what we'd realized recently—the same New York midwife had delivered my Isabel and Julie's son Benjamin. We talked about Brooklyn. Then we read Benjamin's poems. There was one line that seemed like an answer to one of my brother Joey's lines, the second half of a couplet separated by almost twenty years.

Joey: "What is the answer to this ragged eating?"

Benjamin: "There is a loving situation in the kitchen."

Julie said that would make a good broadside.

—

That moment when the past becomes sculptural—there was an instance, and you're no longer in it, you can walk around it. Like an ice sculpture. But it's melting, it's changing.

—

Sylvia Townsend Warner, from *Lolly Willowes*:

She was changed, and she knew it. She was humbler and more simple. She ceased to triumph mentally over her tyrants. . . . The amusement she had drawn from their disapproval was a slavish remnant. . . . There was no question of forgiving them. . . . and the injury they had done to her was not done by them. If she were to start forgiving she must needs forgive society, the law, the church . . . and half a dozen other useful props of civilization. All she could do was go on forgetting them. But now she was able to forget them without flouting her forgetfulness.

—

"Unwitting heiress of generations of bitterness"—Lena, from James Baldwin's *Another Country*

—

Confided in Gigi about the cascade of disaster and humiliation at work and home and everywhere in 1999, 2000, 2001, the truths about my divorce and my family that I never share—

She couldn't understand why I was so ashamed. She said that being arrested for trying to keep your ex-husband from walking away with your little girl while she's screaming, "Mommy, mommy!" is more deserving of a Girl Scout badge than a scarlet letter. "And your parents, frankly, are assholes." I resisted the urge to defend them, to talk about class. She meant well. But I went home more depressed than if I'd said nothing at all.

—

Isabel, away for two nights at Andrew's, comes back and sees me in my new bra and underpants. Clearly hurt: "You never told me you bought those."

I love her sense of ownership of my life. The sweetness, the intimacy.

—

Isabel is at a class sleepover at the Sands' house. They are watching the World Series and running in and out of the house to witness the eclipse. I want the Red Sox to win for my father. Whatever he has done or not done, he's old, and he's waited a lifetime for this.

I'm sitting in Luka's, watching the game, remembering the World Series in 1986, happening as Joey was dying.

In the bar, pandemonium as the Red Sox win, and people are congratulating me because I come from Boston. I laugh and lapse into my accent. I don't even think about it—I just dial home. My father picks right up. For a moment, it doesn't matter that we haven't spoken in years.

"Jesus," he says, "It's like a miracle. All my kids are calling me. I think even Joey tried to call, but we had a bad connection."

Ma still won't talk to me, though I've tried everything. (I even sent her a CD of songs by Dominic Chianese, who plays Corrado Soprano on TV.)

Maybe it's for the best.

2005

Someone I Used to Know

Dreamed I had a broken typewriter and called someone to fix it. The repairman reached into the well of keys and pulled out something that was stuck, and the keys all jumped up to strike the paper. "Here's your problem," he said, holding up a small diamond ring.

—

I never had a diamond or wanted one. Our rings were silver and cost nine dollars each. We bought them at a table on Telegraph Avenue in 1986. Eight years later, when I was pregnant in New York, I lost my ring waiting for the F train. It bothered me a little but Andrew didn't care, so I pretended not to. A month later, on a business trip in London, I bought myself a cheap replacement.

Later, when we went to childbirth classes, the teacher asked the husbands to say why they wanted to be present at the births of their children. "To help with the breathing." "To rub her back." "To count between contractions."

Then it was Andrew's turn. "Like they said."

And finally, there was Mohammed, who was married to an Italian-American girl in the neighborhood who looked a lot like me.

"Mohammed," said the teacher, "why do you want to be there for Donna?"

"Because," he said with a heartbreaking earnestness, "ees miracle."

Andrew laughed, too cool to believe in miracles.

I laughed too.

—

Macy was in town to give a reading. I ran into her at Elizabeth's and invited her over. When she arrived I was washing the floor. She asked if she could use my computer. I turned it on and she laughed as it beeped and buzzed and slowly connected to the Internet.

"You still use dial-up?"

"Yes," I said. "It's cheaper."

"Huh," she said. "I took you for a rich divorcee."

"Sorry to disappoint."

When I finished my housework, I looked up and saw that she was Googling herself. Is that a thing that ambitious young poets do now? Well, good for her. Nobody lights a light and hides it under a bushel basket, right? (Unless they've been raised like me and every girl I knew growing up.) At Isabel's Episcopal school, Chaplain Luther reminds the students that they are the light of the world.

Macy's so sure of herself, so charismatic. I love her laugh. I've always thought I could fall in love with a woman. I could fall in love with her, I bet, if she weren't moving to New York.

From lesbians, I learned how to be a person, not just a woman or a girl. And raising Isabel in a house with no men, I have made some kind of paradise where females are always the most important people in the room.

We walked to a café and sat drinking coffee in the sun, reading the paper. Macy was wearing her wife beater (she calls it) and I could see her tattoos. Her arms are huge. She grinned at me and told me she used to be infatuated with my type—"The kind of women who wear black slips to bed." (How can she tell?)

Anyway, she doesn't believe in monogamous relationships. She believes in orgies. And she doesn't understand this new campaign for gay marriage. Why would anyone want to be married? "What's the point of being queer?"

As we gathered up our things, I saw a familiar face on a page in the *Times* and I grabbed the section of the paper she'd just finished reading, scanning it quickly.

"What are you looking at?" she said, a little suspiciously.

Here he was again. That face, that penetrating look—after all these years, I still couldn't escape him. But this wasn't a review of a play. This was news of August's terminal cancer.

"Oh, nothing," I said, remembering the girl I was when I met him long ago—a superego in a skirt, obsessed with what was wrong and right in all matters racial, sexual, and feminist.

"It's just someone I used to know," I said, crumpling the newspaper and tossing it in the trash.

And then I tried to give Macy all my attention. We talked about John Wieners and Maureen Owen and Anne Waldman—we love Maureen, and, oh God, Anne—and we talked about the Lower East Side in the 1980s. But I was distracted. Was he really dying? And why should it matter to me, anyway?

She was writing something on the palm of her hand with a Magic Marker as we talked. She made a fist, and then she opened her hand like a fan in front of my face and beamed at me, and I saw what she'd written: "SEX," and I laughed.

—

Back in Oakland. The workmen were hammering the siding on our building and it was so hot in the apartment, I drove to Muir Beach to cool off. When I got home I saw that the encaustic painting Young had given me—"To sell when you need money"—had been knocked off my wall. I took out the stepladder to try to rehang it, but it was ruined.

Andrew brought Isabel upstairs to me. We talked about summer plans and he kissed her goodbye. I took two lime popsicles from the freezer and sat on the stepstool. She draped herself on my lap, sucking her popsicle. "Ah," she said, sighing. "The luxury of a woman and a girl."

—

Reading Budd Schulberg's *What Makes Sammy Run*. The virtuous female protagonist, it turns out, had a thing with Sammy, the enemy of respectability and labor solidarity in the novel. She tries to explain it to her platonic friend, a fellow union organizer: "Well, the first time Sammy came into my office . . . I was ready to tear him limb from limb and at the same time I had this crazy desire to know what it felt like to have all that driving ambition and frenzy and violence inside me."

—

My brother Richard called last night. "It's one o'clock here. My cab is the only one on the street at this time of night in Mattapan. What time is it there?"

He tells me that the government and God protect him. Police leave him alone cause his brilliance is well known. If they stop him and go back to their cars and check their radios, they come back and let him go after learning about "all the revenue" he's generated through his "inventions."

"Like the screen behind first base in baseball." He stops to catch his breath. "I invented that."

He's stopped taking his medication. Behind the bravado, I hear the loneliness in his voice, his Boston accent thick and broad. I recognize it as my own.

He says he had a dream about God.

"It wasn't Dad, though he was wearing the same dark jacket and pants."

He says he was protected; said God, his God—I shudder, because now Richard sounds like Dad—will protect him even if it means killing the other person.

Then he tells me about a war dream—or is it a dream? The war is real. We are always at war now.

He says he saw women begging God to stop the bombs dropping from the sky—women dressed like the Blessed Mother, but dusty—and they weren't virgins—and the bombs stopped.

He has to stop talking for a minute to think about that.

"Whose side is God on?" he says. "I know you're wondering. I've thought about that. And I have an answer."

In California, the palms are rustling in the dark. There are rats in the trees. This place is not all it's cracked up to be, but it's my victory. I'm three thousand miles and three time zones away.

I have clocked his monologues. Half an hour or more—nothing to him. I can listen to him for another twenty minutes and still get a good night's sleep as long as I take an Ambien. I adjust my pillows.

"You probably don't think as theologically as I do," he says. "Joey did. We were on the same level."

Silence while we remember Joey, who did everything possible to distinguish himself from us. No shit jobs or Catholic schools for him; he went to an Ivy League college, wore only natural fabrics, loved German lieder, and won a big poetry prize at Columbia. Once, in Riverside Park in 1985, he scoffed at me for worrying about him getting AIDS. He wouldn't get it, he said. He only associated with men from Harvard, Yale, Columbia. A year later he was dying in Lenox Hill Hospital.

"Linda," Richard says, condescending to me, "are you prepared to think theologically?"

Richard, Joey, and Michael were altar boys. Two of the priests they served are now on the list of abusers in Boston. Girls couldn't serve. Couldn't get that close to God.

"Yes, Richard. Sure." I lapse into my Boston accent. "Go ahead. Talk.

2006

Boiling Tea

Andrew took Bel up to Sea Ranch with his family. I woke up at dawn and went to the Y. I was wearing sandals and my hair was a mess and it was pouring rain. I had to park far away. By the time I got to Broadway I was sopping. As I came around the corner, I bumped right into a young brother.

He backed up and looked me up and down, trying to find something, anything, to admire about me, and said politely, "Pretty feet."

I scowled at him. He looked hurt.

He squinted at me in the rain. "I was just trying to be nice."

"I know," I said. "But it's so cold, and I'm so tired."

—

*That day, last October—I was at work and had my headphones on as I
listened to an interview and edited the transcript of an oral history of a*

black theater scholar. It began the way all our interviews begin—with life history. Dr. W., like other interviewees in this series, brought up Emmett Till's murder, without being asked. Remembered seeing the picture in Jet. *At lunch I turned away from my screen and removed my headphones to read some poems by John Weiners—"Billy," and the one about Neponset. I was tired. I hadn't slept the night before. It was as if I were keeping vigil or something, listening to mournful whistles of the trains passing through Jack London Square, across Lake Merritt.*

Then I went back to editing. Dr. W. talked about her work on the anthology of plays by Black women, a book that Vee loaned me in college. Then there was a discussion about Lorraine Hansberry and Lloyd Richards and August that made me think about the news I'd read in the paper. It had been troubling me all month—the way I crumpled the newspaper and thrown it in the trash.

At five o'clock I removed my headphones and clicked to catch up on the day's news. And there was August's face, and his obituary, on the front page of the New York Times, *("above the fold," as they used to say, though now the paper was not paper and there was no crease). He had passed the day before, on October 2nd—same day as Joey.*

I couldn't believe it. I cancelled plans for the night so I could think about it, and then I tried to forget about it. What, after all, did it have to do with me?

And then strange things started to happen—like in his plays—and it was as if I'd been found. At first I resisted—"This is absurd." I hadn't seen him since I was 29. "I'm just not important enough to be haunted."

I couldn't talk about these "co-incidences"—who'd countenance that? Only true believers, and women like me—I was sure there were many—who'd fallen under his spell.

Suddenly I remembered Kathy, my boss in Minnesota; I hadn't thought of her in years. I found her email address; wrote to her. She wrote right back—he'd been haunting her too, she said, and she'd been thinking of me. She hadn't seen him in decades. She remembered the day she introduced me to him. Remembered what I looked like then.

Three times in two days, I heard the Staples Singers' "Samson and Delilah" on the radio:

> Delilah climbed on Samson's knee,
> Said tell me where your strength lies if you please.
> She spoke so kind and she talked so fair,
> Samson said, "Cut off my hair."

and other things happened—things no one would believe—and I began to accept that there were strange forces at work. A restless and busy spirit—visiting all of us? Maybe this haunting was a kind of—nourishment?

RUBY
Get you some good dirt and put seeds in if you want them to grow.

KING
This is the only dirt I got.

King Hedley II

—

Baking gingerbread with stout and molasses, roasting potatoes, sautéing chard with goat cheese and beets—listening to Isabel in the other room—my little girl—still playing with dolls. She has her period. She still has nine baby teeth and is embarrassed when she hears Marvin Gaye's sexy songs.

—

Stanley on the phone last night telling me about a glamorous night out with Susan. "They had wahlay parking." Huh? Oh yes. He means valet.

Last month when I called him he said I must have been picking up his "wibes."

—

Spring's son is on the other side of my back door again having sex with his girlfriend while I read *My Emily Dickinson*. It's not the first time I've

heard them on the landing. Tomorrow I'll find another opaque black con-
dom thrown from the back porch into the driveway.

—

Tonight he's there again, but he's alone. I sit on the couch reading about
Dickinson while he writes rhymes. I can hear him chanting softly, count-
ing beats.

> *The Martyr Poets – did not tell –*
> *But wrought their Pang in syllable –*
> *That when their mortal name be numb –*
> *Their mortal fate – encourage Some –*

—

I've been making collages and writing obsessively and have stopped going
to the gym.

Gigi came over the other night, completely soused. I moved my collages
off the kitchen counter to get dinner ready. She poured herself some wine
and slapped my ass. Then she reached for my chest.

"Gigi!"

She laughed.

"You've gotten fat, girl!" she said. "You can't let yourself go. You need to
find a man."

She's past sixty and naturally skinny. She doesn't have to work at it. (No
wonder her sullen, chubby daughter no longer talks to her.)

I moved to the other side of the counter, stung. I hadn't realized I'd
gained so much weight.

"I've been working really hard," I said. "I'm fighting depression."

She cackled. "No excuses!" she said, and took my face in her hands.
"You're so bee-yoo-tee-ful when you're not fat!"

I know the drill. She won't even remember this exchange. And I'll never forget it.

—

Something's wrong with me. I need to sleep all the time. Maybe that's why I'm gaining weight. I can hardly move. I call Kaiser, try to get help. Nothing.

Can't go on like this. Can't let Isabel down.

Had to sleep on the floor under my desk in the middle of the day.

—

So sick. I can barely walk a block without taking a rest on the curb. Me, a beast of burden—now so weak. The last six or eight years of stress— moving to California, the end of my marriage, eviction and a new place, upheaval at work, travel for work, a new job, breakups (I always walk away)—and money worries, car trouble, betrayals and trauma—I feel like I'm trying to fit my extended nervous breakdown into weekends here and there—when I have some time alone, off-stage—so I can keep my job and take care of Isabel.

I pull my dog-eared copy of Fitzgerald's *The Crackup* off my shelf, thinking, as I have thought many times before, "You can only have a nervous breakdown if there's someone to help you."

—

"Get help, get help"—but where? Whenever there's a tragedy they always quote some psychologist: "They should have gotten help."

Once when Isabel was little I went to a therapist named Lia Lund because her name was on a list I got from my health insurance company. She made me rest on the couch in her home office, which seemed weird, since it wasn't psychoanalysis. And she interrupted our second session to sign for a delivery from Smith & Hawkin. When I wrote her a check for my co-pay she said, "Make it out to Linda Lund." I said, "I thought your name was Lia?" She said, "That's the name I use. But my real name is Linda. I hate Linda."

Now I'm desperate. I can't stop thinking about my great-grandmother in Killarney, the one who died in the madhouse, grieving her dead infant and leaving four other children motherless. I call Kaiser again. They check my prescription and say I should be fine. But I'm not fine. "Maybe I need a new prescription?" No, the things I'm on should work. "But they don't work." More and more phone calls, to no avail. It seems the only way to get any help at all, to break through their wall of cost-containment, is to say I am suicidal. You can get locked up for admitting that. How degrading—to insist that the mother of a small child—me, my mother's daughter—utter those words—

In the windowless room in a beautiful building designed by architect Julia Morgan: Myesha, Tamika, Fiona and Leanne—

Boxes of Kleenex here and there on tables and windowsills—stories of what happened then—and drink, drug, food and sex now—"Narcotics cannot still the tooth"—Dickinson knew—

We go around the circle. Leanne wants to tell us her middle name but she can't say it. Crying, she writes it down and hands it to Myesha.

Myesha reads it aloud: "Obedient."

Leanne says her father named her. And then, when she was six, he started to interfere with her.

My middle name is Ellen, after my father's Irish foster mother.

"I never heard her raise her voice in anger," my father told me many times. Meaning, she was a saint, compared to my mother. Anger, my father often told me, was a sin.

———

I found my mother on the floor under the kitchen table after school one day when I was fourteen. I made the other kids stay outside while I took care of it. When I called my father at work—something that just wasn't done; he was terrified of his bosses, and he didn't like us—I tried to tell him what had happened. He told me to take care of it myself and hung up before I could say another word.

Ma had taken some pills, but I couldn't tell if she was really groggy or was faking it.

She needed attention and she knew where to get it. From me.

———

This building where we sit and talk used to be called "The Home for Incurables." Now we're supposed to have hope.

I try to sum up the story of my life—especially my marriage—in twenty minutes in a one-on-one counseling session. The psychiatrist listens carefully and says kindly, "There's nothing wrong with you my dear. It's just heartbreak. A lifetime of heartbreak."

Then he changes my prescription.

———

A month later and I'm doing better. But everything's messed up. I haven't ruined Isabel, but the rest of my life needs fixing.

On the way home from work I passed a handwritten sign in front of the barbershop: "I can weave a bald head."

If he can weave a bald head, I should be able to make something of my strands, my fragments and my talents and my luck.

———

After vacillating, worrying about money, I decided to travel to Seattle to see August's last play and to visit Vee. It was snowing when I got there, and I happened upon a *feis* in the convention center across from the place where I was staying. I wandered into the Irish step dancing festival and was amazed to see that the best dancers on the stage were not Irish but African American. They were dripping with medals, and everyone cheered for them. Incredible! I remembered the racist Irish Dorchester of my youth, and all the little one-hundred-percent Irish girls I envied then, and I smiled.

It was great to see Vee's face that night—her dimples, and the grey at her temples. I remember how she struggled with the decision to leave her husband and her job at the insurance company, to move west and become an artist—and now she's directing plays and teaching, and she and Kim want to get married.

—

I first met Vee when I helped her on the light board for a production of The Caucasian Chalk Circle *at Holy Cross. One day she invited me to sit at "the Black table" in the cafeteria; I was shy, but I did it. Later, she and her friends invited me to parties. That year we were reading Morrison, Walker, Childress, Shange; no theory. We weren't sophisticated, but we were feminists. And we were nice people. After the dances, we'd go home and get into nightgowns and boil tea and gossip with Shelly and Jennifer. (Hearing them talk about "boiling tea," I finally realized it was an African-American synonym for gossip—what Isaac Bashevis Singer euphemized as "character analysis"—and not just the literal thing we did when we plugged the hot pot into the socket after parties.)*

The big word then was "tolerance." As if white people were supposed to be high-minded if they could "tolerate" difference. But I thought my Black friends tolerated me and what I couldn't help but be.

I was on scholarship, didn't have enough money to buy deodorant or soap; didn't fit in with the rich Irish girls in their Lanz nightgowns and Fair Isle sweaters. One day Vee and I were standing in line in the lobby of the student union. Kevin Moriarty, a senior from a lace-curtain Irish Catholic background, was in front of us. The school belonged to guys like him and his father; they "let us in," the boys would remind us after half a keg.

Vee was smiling, managing him as I'd seen her manage others. Then he made some remark about her "scholarship status" or affirmative action

*or something. Vee laughed and put her arm around me, flipping the
ends of my straight hair.*

"I'm not on scholarship," she said. "But she is."

I smiled. She adjusted the collar of her Izod shirt.

He turned away, speechless.

*I remember how glad I was that Vee had deftly put my whiteness to
good use.*

"Do you remember," we said to each other all weekend in Seattle. "Do
you remember?"

*That June right after we graduated, they rented a house down the Cape.
I couldn't afford to chip in but was included anyway. We went to the
beach and everyone stared at them, the only Black people for miles
around. Sunburned mothers of big families sat at the water's edge in
lounge chairs, turning to give us dirty looks.*

*That night we walked down the dark road to get ice cream, and a car
full of the kind of bullies I grew up with nearly drove us off the road,
laughing and screaming at us—them?—us. After that, my friends de-
cided we'd just hang around the cottage, barbecuing and dancing.*

"Do you remember?"

Yes, I remember.

In Seattle Vee took me to her favorite Mexican place. "Liberal white
people treat me like a spokesman," she said after our third margarita. "I'm
so sick of explaining things to them and having them compliment me on
being 'articulate.' Why don't white people talk about racism with other
white people?"

"Because white people hate a white person who thinks she's better than
they are. And a self-righteous white person is a ridiculous figure every-
where, right? Because maybe she thinks she knows, but what does she
know?"

She laughed.

"I guess that's the risk you have to take," she said.

It's true that fools are my favorite characters in literature. Maybe there is a role for a fool like me.

We talked about love and about Alice Childress's *Wedding Band* and her novel, *A Short Walk*. The character Cora is a little girl, walking with her father Bill, and she calls him 'Papa-la.' He asks her why she calls him that.

> *"One day I heard a fine 'la' sound and then I knew."*
>
> *"Where did you hear it?"*
>
> *"Inside a my head—'laaaaa.'. . . You can laugh if you want . . ."*
>
> *Her father answers: "That's no joke. 'La' is one of the finest things I ever heard anybody relate."*

———

Saturday, taking a short cut to Ashby BART, Isabel and I drove past Bethany Baptist and past Mavis's, the place where I worked in 1986 right after Joey died. I had dropped out of grad school and was working two jobs, saving money to move us back east.

"See that restaurant? I used to be a waitress there," I said.

"Really?"

"Yes. When you're older you can come here and try the food."

———

> *Mavis used to sit at the counter watching me fill the salt and pepper shakers while we waited for church to get out. Her favorite perfume was White Shoulders. I had a vial of it, too.*
>
> *She knew I was in mourning for the brother who'd just died of the dis-*

ease whose name she would not say because it was gay. But right around the corner from the restaurant, at Children's Hospital, there were babies who'd been born with AIDS, and were dying of it. And sometimes they were born addicted to this new drug, crack.

"Baby, you pretty," she said. "Now when they tell you so in here, don't look down. Just smile and thank them for the compliment."

It's true that I was rather stern, not wanting to be taken for a flirt. And of course I was sad. So sad.

But sometimes Irv could make me laugh girlishly, despite myself.

As Mavis talked, he danced past with his broom and winked at me and I smiled. Mavis had told me he'd "been away."

"Where was he?" I asked.

She peered over her glasses at me and didn't answer.

She had told me that I should always answer the phone so Irv wouldn't have to.

"If someone asks where he is, just say you don't know."

Later I heard there was a warrant out on him in Louisiana, and that's why we had to watch out for him. He didn't want to go away again. I had been raised to think the police, like the priests, were God. Always right, and above reproach. Now here were some of the best people I knew, and they knew better.

I got a free meal every shift. Irv would scramble the eggs the way I liked them, then push the plate through the kitchen window. Smiling at my bookishness, he'd watch me eat at the counter while I read. That was nice—having a man feed me.

The first day of work Irv asked me where I was from.

"Boston."

"Irishtown," he said.

I told him that my mother's mother was Sicilian.

"Then you ain't quite white. My uncle was in Sicily in the war. It's almost Africa."

Sometimes a white customer—there weren't too many—would complain about the sweet iced tea. When that happens, Mavis told me, "Don't apologize. Just say, 'That's the way we like it.' Say, 'We like sweet tea'"

After church, the place would fill up with women in beautiful hats, and men would arrive in tracksuits, waiting for the football game to start, ordering eggs, French toast, or pancakes and a choice of sides.

"Would you like ham, sausage, or bacon with that?"

"Yes."

"All of them?"

"Yes."

"Potatoes, grits, or rice?"

"All that and more, baby."

I ran back and forth, carrying twenty-four plates to a table of four men. And then they'd finish off with Mavis's famous pie. (We didn't think about diabetes or anything then. I wonder if those men are still alive.)

One day Andrew came to meet me at the end of my shift. Irv whispered in my ear, "Aw, you say that's your husband? That's not a man, baby— that's a boy." And then he cooked my blue-eyed devil some salmon croquettes.

—

Andrew took Isabel to Yosemite yesterday. Saying goodbye to her I thought my heart would break. I went to get a massage, maybe the fifth or sixth in my life. It's been so long since anyone has touched me. In the car on the way to Piedmont Springs I heard news of the ceasefire in Lebanon. Sounds of a very old woman, buried in rubble, crying for water,

water, water. And then the cries of a woman realizing her husband and son were buried in the rubble. And after that the obscene counterpoint of spokesmen for Hezbollah and Israel. And, worst of all, George Bush talking. Right after the massage began, I broke down on the table. Cried so much I thought my facial features had been rearranged. I must have looked like a woman in a Picasso or de Kooning painting.

Started work on poem called "Trinity" when I got home.

—

In the car with Isabel. Rick James on the radio. "She's a super freak, a super freak, she's super freaky."

Isabel, puzzled, said, "Mom, can being a freak be a good thing sometimes?

2007
Because You Are Full of Rage

Isabel comes and shows me a smidgen of blood on her pad and asks, matter-of-factly, "How's this, mom? Is this about how much there should be on it when I need to change it?"

After she falls asleep I rinse her bloody underpants in the sink.

—

"Among all the enemies of a plebeian writer's promise, none lasts longer than self-pity." —Murray Kempton

It's hard to write about your mother breaking your finger without some self-pity, hard to write about money and divorce and class without sounding maudlin. Maybe someday I'll pull myself up by my bootstraps and become a good writer.

—

A report from a British traveler to Ireland in the 1860s, where so many Irish were homeless, mad, still starving, because there were lesser famines before and after The Great Famine: "I am haunted by the human chimpanzees I saw along the hundreds of miles of horrible country . . . to see white chimpanzees is dreadful; if they were Black one would not feel it so much."

Virginia Woolf wrote home from Ireland: "It is a lovely country, but very melancholy, except that the people never stop talking."

At home I open my book about the holy wells of Ireland and find that Isabel has written her name in it and drawn smiling porpoises on the map.

———

Dinner with Ann the other night. We talked about Beckett and our Catholicism. She remembers her mother having a miscarriage and begging little Ann to baptize the bloody mess in the toilet.

———

Andrew and Isabel go to Safeway and stand in the aisle and talk matter-of-factly about what kind of pads she needs. I cry with gratitude when she tells me about it. No shame in her game.

———

Somewhere, if I could find them, there were some steps, many, many steps, that led to the Blue Bird of Happiness. But I would have to climb them and they sort of just sat in the middle of the sky. It would be worth it, though. I wondered if they were in another city. What city?
—Adrienne Kennedy, *People Who Led to My Plays*

Reading Ferrante's *The Days of Abandonment*—ashamed that I have been as low as that. Permeated by suffering.

"Why does tragedy exist? Because you are full of rage. Why are you full of rage? Because you are full of grief." —Anne Carson

———

Visited Nam in New Orleans. He's down there working as an engineer for FEMA.

We talked about the kids, and how we first met—on a field trip to a pumpkin patch a few weeks after 9/11. He was talking a blue streak in an accent so strong I couldn't understand a word of it. I looked up at him and said, "You're the tallest Asian man I've ever met." He laughed. "I know, I look like J Crew model. Everybody say so."

Four years later, I understand him and his accent perfectly.

It was rainy yesterday. He gave me a tour of the city, then took me to the Lower Ninth Ward. Two years since Katrina and it's still apocalyptic and scarily silent except for the sounds of some water birds.

We walked through the wet grass. He went one way, I went another. Near a collapsed house I found a Bible open to the Book of Job. Since it was about to turn to pulp I took a few pages.

On a board near a ruined Four Square Gospel church, someone had written:

> *Get wisdom! Get understanding! Do not turn away from the words of my mouth.* — Proverbs, 4:05

On another sign in front of a door marked with an X and the number of dead bodies found inside the building after the flood: "Can these bones live?"

Something moved in the grass and I shivered.

Nam had come up behind me. I jumped.

"You scared of a little snake?" He put his arms around me. "You want to hear about scary snakes? Let me tell you about my time in the jungle in the Communist Reeducation Camp."

I'd heard the story a few times since 2001, but I let him tell it again. A story like that, you should be able to tell as often as you like.

On the way back to his SUV he told me about the piece of gold his mother brought him and passed through the fence so he could use it to bribe his way out.

"And I knew just where to put it for safekeeping—up my ass—because I'd read *Papillon*."

On the plane on the way home I finished "Goodness and Mercy" and started writing a new poem called "The Public Gardens."

———

From Raboteau's *Slave Religion*:

> *While white preachers repeatedly urged, "Don't steal," slaves just as persistently denied that this commandment applied to them, since they themselves were stolen property.*

> *"I did not regard it as stealing, nor do I regard it as such now. I hold that a slave has a moral right to eat and drink and wear all that he needs, and that it would be a sin on his part to suffer and starve in a country where there is plenty to eat and wear within his reach."*
> — Henry Bibb

———

Wrote a new draft of "Self Portrait as a Meadow," and read Anne Waldman.

"Not that he held her back exactly. It was a condition of the times. You merged with the man in an imitation of enlightenment."
— from "Feminafest"

———

Always reading the next book as if it would change my life. But now the only thing that can change my life is my own writing, my own art. The renewal of some pacts—abdication of others.

———

Charlie and I had dinner last night at the Sicilian place.

"You know who you look like?" he said.

"Who?"

"Dora Maar. Picasso's mistress."

"Which one was she? Didn't he drive them all to suicide?"

"I think there were a few he couldn't kill."

He talked about Romanticism and a Wittgenstein conference in China and his most recent affair with yet another grateful middle-aged woman. I asked him brightly, "How's your wife?" and he laughed and reached across the table to spear a piece of my squid. Over dessert he listened to me talk about my divorce (*ad nauseam*). I said, "I'll never marry again," and he asked why.

"Maybe I was married to the only person I could ever love. I date, but I always see the end of things in the beginning. Of course," I said, "I'm not a romantic."

He laughed.

"You? You're the ultimate romantic. You're always looking for something that trumps your intelligence and your morals."

—

At *Joe Turner* at the Hansberry Theater in SF with Isabel. First time I've seen one of August's plays where the audience is majority Black. Jack's daughter plays the little girl in this production.

At intermission I'm standing in line for the bathroom and I ask the woman behind me if she likes the play.

She looks over my shoulder at his picture in the program and says, "Yeah, it's pretty good. For a white guy, he sure knows a lot about Black people."

"Oh," I say, "he's not white. His father was white, his mother was Black."

She stares hard at the picture.

"Hmmm."

—

Nuala O'Faolain in *The Story of Chicago May*:

"By leaving, she rejected them before they rejected her. . . . She had exhausted, now, the promise implicit in homesickness."

On writing an autobiography: "But very, very few people do it. And why? Because it is truly laborious. Because it asks for a feat of memory retrieval, and the memories that return may still be full of unease and hurt, or simply resistant to words. . . . Autobiographies are always, perhaps, addressed to the mother."

My Singing Teachers

I
used
to have
heartstrings
but now
down to one,
which works all
the same.

Charles Bernstein

The pure contralto sings in the organ loft,
The carpenter dresses his plank

Walt Whitman

Coloratura

As I see quite a few demoralized coloraturas,
I thought I should write.
A singer needs to feel the ring in her voice
and before the color comes
she may not like the sound.

I've seen singers cry,
the mouth and face stuck.
Now I can tell
from the bathroom down the hall
when it's about to happen.

One student was mistakenly trained as a mezzo.
A very upsetting situation, of course.
This was the first time I had come across this.
Moving the head as if indicating
"yes" or "no" was useful.

I had a really lovely singer, a mature student
who did not know where her passagio was
and another one trained as a lyric.
This kind of instrument when it is young
will tolerate a lot of punishment.

A coloratura who doesn't understand
her middle voice will find that the quality
of the sound is compromised.
Under-singing is never
an answer to the problems.

Work

Franz Kafka, the insurance man who wrote *Amerika*, never went to America. Emily Dickinson stayed home, wrote poems, and baked cakes with her Irish maids. *Mon oncle* Wallace Stevens (also an insurance man) never went to France; in the South during World War I, he saw a train filled with Black troops headed to the war there, and he found their exuberance "absurd." James Schuyler said that people often had the mistaken impression from his subject matter—so many flowers—that he knew a lot about gardening. William Carlos Williams pried mouths open. Frederick Douglass went to Ireland and thought the peasants had it worse than slaves. Walt Whitman was a nurse. Lucia Berlin was a nurse. After writing novels and doing anthropological fieldwork and interviewing former slaves for the Federal Writers Project during the Great Depression, Zora Neale Hurston ended up working as a maid in Florida. Lorine Niedecker was also a cleaning lady. Edith Wharton wrote in bed, dropping her pages onto the floor for the maid to pick up. They say Karl Marx never went into a factory, yet he knew that delicate fabric demanded delicate hands. Hence, silk spun from the blood of little children.

Doris Love

May is lilacs, June is roses, and honeysuckle blooms all summer here. It's grey today, though; February and no valentine.

"What's that on your dress?"

An imaginary flower, big as a baby. Exaggerated.

"It's a design. Nothing, really."

Her new employers love her love of color. They wear only black or grey. They say her dresses are good for babies: "Visual stimulation." She heard Margit on the phone, talking about how well it's going. "A nanny share. Yes, she's from the islands." What islands? Not everyone with a gap-tooth smile is from the islands! She herself never saw the sea until she came to Brooklyn. That day at the Narrows the water was strange, all whipped up, the color of baby shit before the baby's ever had anything but mother's milk. Mustard yellow with blue and green in or under it.

To get off to a good start she took two buses out to the Toys R Us near Coney Island the Sunday before she was to begin work. She wanted to buy two of something for each of her part-time babies. But the store was closed. Nothing but gulls screaming, and a man alone in his car in the parking lot. Or—not alone. A woman's head comes up from his lap.

She waits for the bus back. Some bird makes a small sound in the eaves at the bus stop. Like the sound of someone drinking. She read about primroses and nightingales in her schoolbooks and thought she'd see them in cold places where they spoke English. But there are none here.

When the bus comes to this remote stop, she's the only passenger. The driver, a big fat gal, says "Lo siento mal." What? "I feel bad about the Toys R Us going out of business, and you came all this way."

Now Doris knows how to say "I'm sorry" in three languages.

Nothing to do but think on the way back to Crown Heights. Maybe this would be a good time to change her name? Malinda. Qualinda. Daylinda. Or Veronica. Almost no one knows her here. Better do it fast, before the babies get big enough to call her "Doris." Hard to change anything after that.

Hector Herrera

Herrera has asked for a day off to attend the funeral of his friend Gleason who hasn't died yet but will go soon. They owe you the days but can make it hard.

Dejar ir y dejar a Dios.

He keeps an extra shirt in his locker with mints and a roll of quarters and a jar of nickels.

There were tampons in the bottom of the locker when he got the job, and they're still there, under his clean socks and underwear. Also some old hand sanitizer, which may not be clean because it was hers.

Una dia a la vez, si, but sometimes you have to plan. Exact change will make things easier when the time comes. Two buses and a long walk along the frontage road. Gleason is dying locally but wants to be buried in a suburb where his ex-wife can't find him. He's the only one who doesn't know that she's forgotten him. Herrera and the priest, who's also in the program—no one else will mourn Gleason. Vivir y dar vivir. Die and let die.

Twice a Finalist

She can no longer write without a computer or come without a vibrator, but she is learning to knit, and this week, inspired by a long piece in the food section of the *Times*, she pickled the first vegetables she ever grew from seed, cucumbers that did surprisingly well on the terrace in pots. She did it while her youngest daughter nursed her baby at the kitchen table, and everything came out good.

She used to correct her own mother for saying that about the bread, the lasagna, the eggplant, funerals, and the coloring in the coloring books: "Ma, you don't say 'It came out good.' You say 'It came out *well*.'" Or you say, "Va bene," like professors do after they return from sabbatical in Tuscany.

Now that her mother is gone she is more relaxed. And her daughters don't correct her. Donna Alessi-Miller, PhD. They know she knows how to say things right when she wants to.

For days, her fingers smelled of vinegar, which bothered the baby and made her feel like she was pickling her knitting. She kept sniffing her hands the way she used to sniff her fingers after writing furiously in her notebooks when she was a girl. She loved the smell of ink, the stuff that used to make her mother sick.

Meditations in Another Emergency

"What's that on your arm, a flower?"

"No."

"A heart?"

"No."

"What is it?"

"It's a rose *and* a heart. I call it 'Rosebeat Ambulette.'"

"Like you Missy Elliot! You Lil' Medic!"

Shrug.

"You didn't tell me you were getting a tattoo. That's hella pretty.
Who drew that? You?"

"Yeah, me."

"You do good roses."

•

Audio figure eights
Sirens looping
Disappearing
In the database

•

I mean: the distance.
I mean: the streets.

•

Eights are infinity. Isn't that funny?
Why not Thee?
Or a driveway?

●

She used to guard a painting, not every day but some days every year
for a few years on rotation. Boring.

They say he painted the first naturalistic path and sky but they still
aren't sure who "he" was.

Thinks of pink if she thinks of it at all. And saints.

●

Thou sayest I should be grateful for a job with benefits and time to
do my nails in the meat wagon.

I say: I saved your life.

●

"The awful consequence of perspective: the vanishing point."

●

Hoses bandages precautions—

No need—no pulse.

Palms sweating

keys, pennies, batteries.

His sweat weighs more than he does.

"Put on your mask."

●

"Can sweat infect you?"

"No. That was on the test. Didn't you take the test?"

•

"Poor guy" is something

we do not think.

•

That last one was beyond obese.

Fries and licorice in puke.

You wish it were funny.

It would be funny, if he were trying to pass you in a hurry in the candy aisle.

•

You're not supposed to eat in the vehicle or talk with the bystanders or use the (generic) sanitary skin wipes to clean the bench in the back. Don't stick little round pink Band Aids one on top of each other in an attempt to make an inch-high sculpture on the dashboard when you're bored. In fact, you're not even supposed to have that box (trademarked) in the vehicle. And never drive down dead-end roads without police backup. A cul-de-sac can be a trap.

•

We stop for hot dogs.

"Is it grisly or grizzly?"

•

Just call it disgusting.

•

We stop for gas.
"Is it pail or pale?"

•

It's a bucket.

•

We stop at the morgue.
"Is it diseased or deceased?"

•

Just say dead.

•

Death is more like a three than an eight.
Or like the letter E.
Me without em. You without me.
Meat without at.
At without F.
An upside-down V:
Keep going until you become part of the horizon.

Prayer (I Have No Money)

Volcanoes be in Sicily

Emily Dickinson

My ATM card doesn't work. Stupid bank. I have no money but I do have time (I can see the minute hand from here), and I have subway fare. Disgusted, I head up to the Met because it's free to look. On the uptown 4: Jeweled belt on boy's hips, buckle with Christ on cross. On a tote bag: "Jesu why are we not perfect?" On that fat boy's T-shirt: "In Memory of Christopher 'Big Pun' Rios." Reminder: Some people don't have money or a job, or they're dead. Old bottles at the museum: If it's here, it's valuable. What of the shitty has survived? Was there much shitty then? I visit my favorite painting, I genuflect. I love that pink behind the cross and in the wounds. Which banker "donated" this painting? Oh, right—Lehman. But all I can think about is Keshia, the service representative at my bank in California. 1-800-USE-LESS! And I said so. How could I? I mean, don't I know better than to rage at her? Christianity, capitalism, female solidarity, the history of slavery. And plastic, and stupid jobs like mine and hers. And anger management, and the middle way—God help me, even though I don't believe in thee.

"Work"

Often, simply moving
a shrub or rose bush
to a summer environment
may cause it to be
expansive in its growth
and so change its status.

White-flowered "Sally Holmes,"
for example.

Doll Values

Always following disaster. Even when I was a kid. Long stories, believe me. Several steps behind damage. When a mother says keep your eyes on them and she goes on dumping potatoes in the water she probably doesn't know you will go on watching them for the rest of your life. As if anything could make you stop.

Eileen Myles

1

Sitting in Café Mogador, waiting for Isabel and Eileen, I take out my newspaper.

2

There were too many people on the pleasure boat that night on the Long Island Sound.

The little girl had decorated her room with butterflies and elephants so there were butterflies and elephants on her coffin.

3

Here's what they do with the rotting carcasses of horses: a truck picks them up, maggots and all. "They go into ladies' cosmetics," says the man who shovels the mess into a truck. "Lotions and creams." Grease and horror redeemed, churned into beauty butter.

4

This week in death: Don Cornelius, Mike Kelley, Dorothea Tanning, Wisława Szymborska. And that little girl and the boy on the boat.

The kids were watching Fourth of July fireworks on a boat named the Candy 1. There is no Candy 2.

I suddenly realize I don't really believe that women die, so they can't escape suffering.

5

Isabel arrives wearing a plaid polyester skirt, not what she was wearing when she left the house in Brooklyn this morning. She looks sheepish and beautiful and sweaty, and she smells like the thrift store. The skirt is too big for her so she's rolled it at the waist.

She keeps coming home from the Goodwill with clothes that might have been my clothes in the 1980s. One day she brought home a crop top that looked just like what I wore at my brother's deathbed.

6

Eileen comes and locks her bike with a heavy chain. It takes a long time, the chain rattling like something in a dungeon.

She's so handsome. Her teeth. And she sounds like everyone I grew up with. The way I still sound when I read aloud to children.

The first time I met Eileen, seventeen years ago, in a gallery, I was newly pregnant with Isabel. I was kneeling to get something out of my bag and I looked up and Susan introduced us. "Have you met Eileen? Linda's from Boston too."

I remember the blue rayon dress I was wearing that night. It cost $45.00 at Street Life on Broadway. A lot of money for me. It was shorter than the dresses I usually wore. It made me feel so pretty. I wore it in Italy with my husband early in my pregnancy.

Annunciations, nativities, last suppers and crucifixions, depositions, res-urrections, assumptions and ascensions. A few Magdalenes. And, on St. Joseph's Day, the Pietà.

I looked at a hundred Madonnas in that dress. I became a Madonna in that dress.

By the eighth week, it was too tight for me. Later, in California, after I lost so much weight, I took it out of storage. It had a low neckline that I could pull down when I needed to nurse.

7

Joey was a snob. You couldn't eat candy or fried food in front of him without being criticized. In the polyester era he wore only cotton, wool, or cashmere; no blends. Not even when he worked as a bar boy at Studio 54, when he wore those tiny pin-striped cotton shorts that shocked me.

One night we arranged to meet down here to go to the Public. I arrived eating Starbursts two at a time. "How can you eat those?" he said. "It's like eating a *candle* or something!" In all the old pictures, he has positioned himself next to me and I'm ignoring him. He had looked up to me. Now he was ashamed of me.

I gave the rest of my candy to a homeless man lounging in front of Cooper Union, making a little show of my tenderness. Joey just kept walking. I had to run to catch up with him.

It was always like that with him—like I might never see him again. And then one day I never saw him again.

8

It's the longest day of the year or feels like it. Why do we get this much time? The light angles into the cavern of the street, it's in their eyes and they can't see me. I watch them while they eat. My writer, my daughter. "My tiny, tiny my-ness."

What You Can't Do About It: Journals

2008

Johnnie

At the Y Maggie and I sat in the hot tub after I cleaned it with a wad of toilet paper. There's always grime around the rim.

"They don't give a shit about us here," she said in that gravelly voice I love.

Things are always broken and dirty in our locker room.

"Do you think it's like this in the men's locker room?" I asked.

"How would I know?" she said. "I stay away from men."

She's 71 years old and does freelance hospice nursing for even older women. This week her favorite patient died.

"Baby, I can't take much more of this at my age. And I don't need the money. I got a pension and Social."

She talked about her mother who died of cancer before she could move back to Louisiana like she wanted to. Maggie nursed her, too.

As I climbed out of the hot tub she looked frankly at my curves and said, "You got it, baby. You look like I used to look when I was young."

Young? I'm 48. Strange to think that someday I might look back and think of these as salad days, despite my fat thighs and cellulite and the creases on my forehead.

Maggie looks like Billie Holiday would look if she'd lived to old age. Beautiful and tough.

She climbs up out of the tub behind me. "That's a pretty bracelet," she says. "Is it ivory?"

"Oh, God, no. It's plastic. I bought it at H&M for $5.00."

"I love ivory. I used to work at an engineering firm and there was a man there who would bring me ivory things from Africa."

She was married once, long ago.

"Nothing in it for me," she once told me, dismissing the institution, and maybe men in general, with a wave of her hand.

—

I don't even look at men at the gym. But there is this one man—it's not like he's the handsomest man—except to me—

I've never talked to him, yet I feel like I recognize him. Like I've been expecting him.

He's like a character in a play—my play—or one of August's plays—the kind of man around whom the world revolves—once a writer notices him.

He's not too tall—maybe 5'10"? Keeps to himself, but I notice that other men acknowledge him with respect and that makes me wonder who he is, what he does, what he thinks. I saw him talking with a meter maid in the street on Tuesday, listening carefully to everything she said.

Yesterday I saw him walking in the pool (I'd never seen him in the water before). I noticed that he had a thick waist. Well into middle age, we were the young people in the lane where the old folks did their exercises.

I stood at the shallow end, watching him as he touched the far wall. As he made his turn, he looked up and noticed me and quickly looked down.

Not a player.

I passed him in the lobby last week but he didn't notice me.

Twice I've passed him on my bicycle as he ran around the lake. Both times I rang the bell on my bike to scatter the geese in my path, hoping he'd look up. The second time, he did. He nodded. I nodded back, but he had already looked away.

—

Today I was sweating hard after my work out. I took the side stairway down to the locker room. I was bolting down the steps when I practically crashed into him as he was running up. We backed away from each other as if we'd been burned. Looked down.

"Excuse me."

"Sorry."

And we kept moving in opposite directions.

—

On the street, I see him and his vanilla cloud of a car, his new-model Dodge. He's often bent over his trunk. At the top of the stairs, in front of the door to the Y, I lean on the railing and look down at him. He seems to keep an entire wardrobe in that trunk—a hat, shoes in shoe trees, pressed shirts, an extra suit. And his Bible. He doesn't notice me.

—

This week he was on his back on the bench doing sit ups when I walked into the weight room. Wanda walked by and we talked a little bit about her chronic pain. Then she left and I was alone with him. I picked up the 15-pound weights. He sat up on the bench. I said "Hi" and he said "Hi."

I said, "I'm Linda."

He said, "My sister's name is Linda." He hesitated and looked at me warily. "I'm Johnnie."

There was an awkward pause. I said, "Is the men's locker room dirty?"

He looked startled.

I laughed and explained myself. "The women's locker room is filthy, and we've been wondering about the men's."

He said, "Yeah, it's the same. But I've seen worse. I bring my own towelettes to wipe things down in there."

"Well," I said, "nice to meet you. See you around." And then I went up to the mezzanine to the exercise bikes.

—

Now if he's in the weight room and I ignore him, he'll make a little show of grunting with exertion, or he'll drop the weights on the floor to get my attention. I laugh. He smiles. He goes his way. I go mine.

I watch him out of the corner of my eye. I never see him flirt with anyone or stare at a woman's ass when her back is turned. Yesterday we talked again. I was nervous. I'm never nervous around men. I don't really know what I said; something about Isabel. He told me that he has no children. He wife is older than he is and by the time they met it was too late.

He told me that he'd had a baby when he was younger, when he was messed up, using crack and heroin, still cycling in and out of Santa Rita and San Quentin. But the baby died. It had happened before Isabel was born.

I wondered how the baby had died, but it was almost as if he was talking to himself and not to me, and he didn't elaborate.

"I'm sorry," I said.

He went into a kind of reverie. "Maybe it's not too late. I mean, my cousin Dante went home to Arkansas and found a girl and had a baby last year and he's older than I am."

He snapped out of it and frowned at me as if I were now implicated in this fantasy. He got up and went to lift a stacked bar that was too heavy for him at first. But he pushed to exhaustion, groaning, ignoring me or performing for me, I wasn't sure which. I went downstairs to swim and think about him.

Leaving the gym, I passed a guy I always notice in the weight room. He looks like an African American Irish man, almost like a leprechaun, except he's dignified. He's short, light-skinned, red-haired, and freckled.

He usually wears T-shirts printed with the names of historically black colleges and universities or the words "Success Through Sacrifice."

In the lobby I heard an older man say to him, "You are a very lucky man," and it was clear that they were talking about a woman. I pictured a trophy, a cliché, a blonde.

—

On the way out of the building last night, as I turned the corner, I saw Johnnie's parked car. He was at the wheel, writing something on a pad of paper. I slowed down on the sidewalk on the passenger side. He looked up. I hesitated, then leaned down to talk to him through the window. "Sistah Big Bones" was playing on the radio.

"I love this song," I said.

He turned it down. He was nervous. An ad for Sleep Train Mattresses came on.

"They hire my guys," he said.

"Hmmm?"

"They hire guys on parole to deliver mattresses."

"Oh! I didn't know that. I knew they did things for foster kids."

"Yeah, and most of them kids got parents locked up. Another form of slavery. Breaking up families."

Now Tony! Toni! Toné!'s "I've Been Thinking of You" was playing on the radio.

"See you soon," I said, backing away.

He started his car and revved it and drove down the block and made a U-turn. As he passed me he smiled and tipped his cap. Then he turned the corner.

—

In the car last night with Isabel, two guys pulled up alongside us and started flirting with us. I'm almost fifty, she is thirteen. So weird.

—

On the sidewalk in the sunshine on Saturday, Johnnie sees me. He shields his eyes and watches me walk toward him. I smile.

"I want you to have this." He shakes his head as if he's not sure he wants to give it to me. And then he shoves it into my hand and walks away.

Later I read the notes on the box. It's a DVD about Johnnie's work with people on parole, people who are home but not yet free. He works for the mayor's office and teaches anger management to men just out of prison.

After Isabel fell asleep I watched it. There he is, talking to a roomful of black men and women just released from prison; now he's at a recovery meeting with a group of people of all races. Next he's doing the scared-straight thing, telling a bunch of sullen young men about heroin and crack and cavity searches in prison, walking back and forth at the front of the room, bouncing on the balls of his feet like a boxer. There's a touch of the preacher in him, and a touch of the poet; at one point in the middle of a speech of one- or two-syllable words and straight talk, he says "here-tofore" with great relish, and I laugh. "Heretofore," his rhetorical flower.

Sometimes his voice cracks with emotion or like something's wrong with his throat. At one point, hamming it up for the cameras, he accidentally spits, and he seems to laugh at himself, his over-the-top performance, and then he wipes his mouth and continues without missing a beat.

The documentary's not just about him, but his story is a through line. They interview an older couple, white people who hired him to work at their gas station when he was just out of San Quentin, trying to get clean. They trusted him and that made all the difference. They gave him the key to the place when he had nothing but the clothes on his back and a trail of mayhem and loss behind him. He found Jesus and built his life up from less than nothing, and he met the older woman who would become his wife, who gave him hope. She saved him. He's devoted to her, and grateful, and sincere when he talks about her.

The film was made a few years ago when he'd been out of prison for about twelve years. They used to tell him to bend over and spread his cheeks; now he has insurance, he's got a home, he's respected. He's proud of his car, his suits, the little place they bought in Hayward. He rose from the dead with the help of God and others. There's his humility, his integrity. And his style. In one speech he mentions his annuity. He likes the word annuity so much, he says it twice. It's poetry.

He's about five years older than I am—must have been almost forty when he finally got clean.

He was starting his new life just as I got pregnant with Isabel.

———

I told myself I was "trying out" my new dress in advance of Amy-Lynn's wedding. So I was wearing heels and that almost-off-the-shoulder number when I ran into him in the lobby.

I said I liked the DVD. "Do you want it back?" I reached for it in my bag. He shook his head. Of course, I was glad to keep it. I said, "I want to learn more about your work. Maybe we can go out for tea some time."

He leaned back, looked me up and down, and said frankly, "Baby, if you and me ever go out, we're gonna be doing more than drinking tea."

Flattered, and exposed for being coy, I blushed.

He was just being honest. He's married. He's not a player. He never would have looked twice at me if I hadn't put myself right in his path.

So we won't be going out for tea or anything else.

———

The gods must be toying with me. Or maybe it's August—didn't I pray to him to send me someone to love? Trickster. Sending me a conundrum, a comeuppance. So much for my sexual probity and moralism and respectability. If Johnnie weren't married, I'd walk down to City Hall with him tomorrow afternoon and get a license.

At the water fountain in the gym, I hear a voice in my ear, a sweet growl. It's Cleo. I haven't seen her in a while. Her daughter goes to school with Isabel. Together, last year, Cleo and I taught a six-week class to the third grade to fulfill our volunteer hours at the school. She's also a single mother.

"Oh, hey!" I said. "Great to see you."

"I was checking you out and I said to myself, that is a fine-ass white woman, and then I realized it was *you*."

"Thank you, Cleo. You look great."

"Oh, yeah," she says, gesturing toward her slender legs and slapping her little butt. "White dudes love me. But the men I want like what you got."

She looks like a model, thin and elegant. She's about ten years younger than I am. Grew up in Clarksdale, Mississippi, and works at Kaiser in the billing department.

She grabs my ass and I laugh.

"You know," I say, "it's a good thing you turned out beautiful, being named Cleopatra and all. Because it could have been awkward for everybody if you were named Cleo and turned out ugly."

She laughs and tells me a joke from the "Queens of Comedy" DVD about aspirational baby names and an ugly toddler named Denzel. I've seen it—Wanda gave it to me for my birthday.

We talk about another stand-up routine on that DVD. The one about getting dickmatized.

"No, no, no."

"To be avoided!"

"Never gonna happen."

On the other side of the stairwell Johnnie is talking about something

136

serious with a haggard-looking white guy and trying mightily not to look my way.

But then our eyes meet.

I turn to give Cleo my complete attention.

—

I need to focus, to read and write, but I can't concentrate. Last night I thought I spied an emoticon in *The Complete Poems* of Marianne Moore. The other day I found a rose petal in my cleavage when I got to work. I have no idea where it came from. I haven't been near roses.

—

Two days later I'm in the back hallway at the Y, a place no one ever goes, and I run into him. We stop and look at each other.

"You're a good woman," he says.

"You're a good man."

He goes upstairs and I keep going down.

—

Isabel in lumberjack plaid shirt and wreath of artificial flowers—she and Elizabeth made wreaths while I was out—so beautiful and Sapphic, it breaks my heart.

—

I see him lifting weights and I take my exercise mat into the corridor where he can't see me and I can't tempt him. I stretch out next to the window that overlooks Torchio's Brake Shop with its retro sign, a 1940s cartoon of a cat screeching to a halt under the question: "Can you stop?"

—

Apparently not. Last week I crossed a line, telling him, when I ran into him in the lobby, that I'd be across the street at Luka's on Friday after 7. He said he might stop in.

I wasn't surprised, was kind of relieved, when he didn't show up. I am not *a mala femmina*—I'm Isabel's mother.

Still, I was hurt, and I felt stupid.

—

Next time I saw him I was getting out of my car across the street from the gym after work. It was dark and cold and rainy. I had a shawl over my head. He got out of his car and our eyes met. I looked away. He ran across Broadway in the rain to apologize for standing me up—"Oh, baby"—and almost got hit by a truck. I turned and walked away.

Now every time he sees me he tries to talk with me but I ignore him. I must have lost my mind to let myself fall in love with a married man. He didn't seduce me, he didn't mislead me. It's nobody's fault but mine.

I'm just going to keep to myself from now on. And write about something other than Johnnie.

—

But now everything's about Johnnie. The Book of Psalms, the Song of Songs and all sorts of music, the little boy and girl flirting shyly in the pew at African American culture night at St. Paul's, and the poems I write in which he never appears. Can a man be a muse?

—

On the way to work I see a little girl on the corner of Telegraph and Hearst holding a seashell to her ear: "Wow, how does it do that without batteries?"

Her brother grabs it and holds it to his ear: "I hear a toilet flushing."

—

At the taqueria in Montclair today, one of the Mexican laborers came in with a shopping list written faintly on a scrap of wood from the construction site. The men in line look like gods with noble noses and scuffed shoes and plaster in their hair.

—

At Walden Pond Books, a guy down on his luck is trying to sell books—battered guides "for Dummies" and a beautiful old volume with embossed covers.

The seller holds the book up. "Would you take something like this?"

"Sure, I like to keep a Q'uran or two around when I can."

—

I parked near the Alzheimer's care home and walked around the lake. When I got back to my car the shift was changing. Workers leaving the garage were trying to get out of there so fast, they almost killed two runners coming off the path around the lake.

At the gym I saw Johnnie coming down the steps as I walked up. I turned away to say hi to Maggie.

—

I have no appetite, I'm losing weight. I think about him all the time.

In the locker room, Wanda compliments me on my waist. "Enjoy that while you have it," she says. "After menopause, it's all downhill."

—

Now, at the Y, I notice things I didn't notice before. I mean, among the men. I've always noticed what we women do for each other here. The men too have their ministry of attention and respect—discretion and candor and warmth. Brotherly love.

—

Isabel's friends are having their bar mitzvahs so every few weeks there's a party. I bought myself an H&M wrap dress, size ten, and a new pair of patent leather pumps from Payless. I'm going to dance my way out of my constrictions.

Isabel and I went swimming at the gym on Saturday, laughing our heads off in the water, hugging and clowning our way around the pool. Then we got dressed to go to Nate's party. At the counter near the sinks, she borrowed my lipstick; first time she's ever worn makeup.

Johnnie was coming up the street as we left the gym. He was in his grey sweats, finishing his run around the lake.

He looked down, expecting me to ignore him. But this time I couldn't. This time, ignoring him would have seemed cruel or disrespectful. I stopped and said, "Johnnie," and he looked up warily. "This is my daughter Isabel. You've heard me talk about her."

"Isabel," he said, his voice cracking, "pleased to meet you."

He looked so happy and relieved. I felt a weight fall off my back.

"You know your mother is the most beautiful woman in the world, don't you?"

"Yes," she said, smiling shyly at him. "I know."

—

That night at the door of the reception hall, Nate's mother told me she planned to seat me with her colleagues from the sickle-cell unit at Children's.

"You'll be next to my friend Eve, who's going through a terrible divorce. I think you'll give her hope. You're the happiest divorced mother I know. And Isabel's happy, too. You must be doing something right."

—

The next time I see Johnnie, we're surrounded by the other regulars in the weight room. Not too many women lift weights, and there's only one who lifts more than I do. When I was younger and shyer, I'd only work out in the women's area of the gym. But now that I'm almost fifty, it doesn't matter. I can even call a young man "honey" without giving him the wrong idea.

"Hi, Johnnie."

"Linda."

"I'm sorry I was cold, Johnnie. You hurt my pride when you didn't show up, and I felt like a fool. But I had no business, I try to be a good person."

"You are a good person," he says. He looks around the room at the men lifting weights.

He says, "You know, I see how these guys respect you. And you know why they respect you? Cause you don't need nothin' from them. Men respect that."

He walks away, like a boxer about to hit the bag.

—

The following week I'm on the way into the gym and he bumps into me in the doorway as he's looking over his shoulder, talking to the janitor. I brush past, smiling. He catches up with me downstairs as I'm about to open the door to the women's locker room. Hello, how are you, fine, fine, fine. Something comes over me, and I mention that I'm going to a matinee in Jack London Square on Friday at 1:15, to see a movie about Boston and my kind of people. If he's not busy, maybe he can meet me there. I walk into the women's locker room without waiting for an answer.

I don't know what got into me, to tell him that. I know he won't come. But this time, when he doesn't show up, I won't feel like such a fool, because I believe he could love me.

—

On Friday, a beautiful fall day, I went to the theater. The trailers started. No Johnnie.

Then, just as *Gone, Baby, Gone* began, I saw his silhouette in the doorway. He took off his cap, looked for me in the dark, hesitated, and took the steps two at a time to sit down next to me. The theater was nearly empty except for two women who came in late and sat right in front of us.

For a while I tried to watch the movie—scenes of the streets where I grew up, the triple-deckers that I know so well, scenes of white people neglecting their children and Black and white detectives trying to find a missing white girl. We stared straight ahead, not touching each other. When he finally kissed me, I braced my leg against the seat of the woman in front of me and she turned around to give me a dirty look.

—

We left and walked to his car in the parking garage. We sat looking out at the cranes at the Port of Oakland until it was almost dark. I told him that those people in the movie were my people, and I kind of missed them. His people, he said, were from Bearden, Arkansas, where you could be lynched because of a white woman. He talked about heroin and decades of degradation, and said something about faith and valor, and then looked embarrassed. But it didn't sound vainglorious to me, and I didn't laugh.

I could hear the Arkansas in his accent; I'd lived in Oakland long enough to be able to distinguish Texas from Lousiana, too, in the accents of the children who'd come to California to escape Jim Crow.

Some people could do whatever they wanted in this life. We were not those people.

It was time for me to go get Isabel from school.

I put my hand on his heart and said goodnight. He put his forehead against mine and we sat like that for a while before I opened the door and walked down the ramp of the garage to my car.

—

It felt like a beginning—like love—because I had somehow made myself real to him. It wasn't about lust. It was about recognition. But I knew this was no beginning—it was the end.

I avoided the gym for five days.

Then, on Thursday, we ran into each other on the stairs.

His face was drawn, as if he hadn't slept. He glowered at me and shook his head. "I broke ALL the rules for you. All the rules."

The rules about marriage, the rules about white women.

"I know," I said glumly. "I did too."

He dropped his stance and his face crumpled.

"I've hurt a lot of people in my life," he said. "A lot of people. Now I try to live in a way that doesn't hurt people I love. Or anyone else."

"Me, too," I said. "I take responsibility."

"I know," he said. "I know you do. That's the kind of woman you are."

"I'm ashamed," I said.

"I ain't ashamed," he said, narrowing his eyes. "And I ain't sorry."

"Me neither," I said.

Because I love you.

And because this is the end of it.

—

I've told June about Johnnie. She's had tons of affairs and she's not judgmental like I am. Yesterday I confided in her about our afternoon at the movies and she congratulated me on crossing the Rubicon, vicariously thrilled at the prospect of hours of passionate love. "Oh, that frisson I remember well!"

"Oh, no," I said, surprised that she thought this was the beginning and not the end. "It was one of the most beautiful days of my life, but it's over. Anything we'd do now would involve sneaking around and lying and disrespecting his wife, and I can't do that."

Can't she see that there's a special place in hell for a white woman who'd tempt a Black woman's man? I know I wouldn't like the company there.

But of course, June is not the one who's doing anything wrong. I am. I've already crossed a line. And I shouldn't be talking with anyone at all about it.

—

Without talking about it, Johnnie and I each changed our schedules so we wouldn't see each other as much at the gym or at the lake. When we did run into each other, we barely nodded. Then one day I saw him in the corridor and he told me that he'd bought the DVD of *Gone, Baby, Gone* and had watched it three times.

I was shocked.

"You look like her," he said shyly, referring to the beautiful lead.

"Oh, no, I don't," I said, embarrassed. "But that's sweet of you to say."

I walked away trembling.

—

I have to change my life.

I've been doing volunteer work for years at Isabel's school because it's part of the contract we signed when we accepted financial aid, and I feel I should be grateful. I like working with the kids but I don't fit in with most of the parents. Not everyone is rich, not by a long shot, but I do stand out when I drop Isabel off in my ancient Volvo with the missing grille. I'm like a toothless woman at a fancy party of BMWs and SUVs. At the last parent party, where I sat listening, once again, to the small talk about kitchen renovations and second homes, I almost blurted out that my mother used to work as a deodorant tester to pick up a little extra money. That would have been a conversation stopper.

Now that Isabel will be starting high school, I've volunteered to be an advocate for youth in the foster care system. My paying job is lonely and I spend most of my time editing the life histories of elite white men. I can't get my boss to give me full-time work, and maybe that's for the best. I can dedicate my Fridays to this other work. And meet some people like me.

———

At the beginning, all the volunteers wanted to work with cute little kids, but it was made clear that it's teenagers who need advocates. Ideally, they told us, boys in the system would have "strong male role models" as court advocates. They told us that advocates often show up once or twice, then disappear when they realize they can't be saviors like in the movies. I looked around the room, counting the other white women, thinking about all the ways that do-gooders do bad.

I was sworn in last week as an officer of the court. They assigned me a case, a seventeen-year-old boy named Marcus, and I met with his attorney. The next week we went out to East Oakland to meet him and his grandmother, who is his legal guardian. Turns out they live near Havenscourt, where Johnnie went to school. But it's not exactly the kind of case we were trained for, since Marcus is not just in the foster care system—he's also in the criminal courts, on probation for receiving stolen goods on his birthday (a friend gave him an iPod as a gift). At least, that is the official charge; actually, he was arrested because the police harassed him and he sassed them back.

His grandmother, who's formal with me, says Marcus is good at math and also art. I promise to get his report cards so he gets credit toward the GED. I call her "Mrs. Williams" though she's only ten years older than I am, still working full-time at a daycare. And that's all I can say about it, as we're not allowed to talk about the cases. Except, I guess, in my notebook, where no one will ever see it.

"Emancipation," they call it when a kid ages out of the foster care system. What a cruel misuse of the word. Most of the kids have nowhere to go but the streets and prison once they're "emancipated."

—

I went home and re-read the social worker's reports. I have in my files the same type of report about my father and his mother, who was an unmarried immigrant suspected of being a fallen woman. Those reports, from 1932, are filled with judgments (and misogyny). In the reports about Marcus's family, the language is more opaque.

On Friday I met Marcus at Lanesplitter Pizza on Telegraph. He towered over me in the doorway but looked scared. His eyes were bloodshot from stress. He was in a shelter until they found his grandmother and she took him in. We sat in the corner and talked a little about his tiny, ferocious attorney and his upcoming court dates.

"Look," I said, "they know they're supposed to send you a strong Black male role model, but I was the closest thing to it this week."

What a stupid thing to say.

He laughed. "I don't mind."

His mother is fourteen years older than he is; I am thirty-one years older. Nice and old.

I took out some colored markers while we waited for our food, and Kareem, who grew up in the projects in Dorchester and often waits on me and Isabel, brought us some paper. And since it wasn't busy, he sat down to draw with us.

—

On Friday afternoons, I pick Marcus up and we drive down International Boulevard, doing errands, going to see the social worker, getting food.

I don't talk about my life. We're not supposed to blur the boundaries while we're working in the system. He doesn't know where I live or work, or whether I'm a mother.

He tells me about his sister, who already has kids. He says if he had a little girl he'd call her "Vodka."

"And if I had twins, I'd call them Caffeine and Gasoline."

—

At the gym after another demoralizing day at work, I was getting my things out of the trunk on a dark street and suddenly there was a man right behind me. "Excuse me, ma'am—"

I recognized him. I've given him money before. I said, "Jesus, don't sneak up on me like that! That's not right."

"Are you scared of me?"

"YOU should be scared of ME. I had a bad day at work and I'm in the mood to take it out on someone."

He smiled a toothless grin and pointed at my pink crystal pendant. "Yeah, I can see you're a witch. A GOOD witch."

I laughed.

"That's nice, too," I said, pointing at the ankh around his neck as I dug into my pocket.

On the car radio on the way home I listened to D'Angelo singing "Devil's Pie":

> Ain't no justice
> Just us

—

Saw Johnnie walking the track with a very serious-looking boy. He stopped to introduce me to his nephew, Jeremiah. They walked on and I turned to watch them and wonder again about Johnnie's baby.
Johnnie's mother used to go to Bethany Baptist, he told me. She died while he was in prison and never had a chance to see the man he became. I wonder if I ever waited on her at Mavis's when I worked there after Joey died, in those awful months in 1986 and '87.

—

Dinner on Friday at Rudy's with Marcus. We parked near Pixar. Everyone had gone home for the weekend. The fence surrounding the office buildings was covered with a thousand big pink roses, so perfect and uniform that they looked like something out of a Disney movie. I reached up to pick a rose and Marcus deftly took my hand before I had a chance to pluck anything. He stepped up his pace, pulling me along toward the restaurant.

"What's wrong?" I said. "There are so many of them."

"I'm on probation," he said. "You pick that and I'm the one they'll arrest." He pointed to the police car at the corner. I hadn't noticed it.

—

In my dream last night, Johnnie and I were in the Home Depot parking lot on a grey Sunday morning, waiting for the store to open so we could get something we needed—a faucet or a fixture or some sponges. We were just sitting in the front seat of his car talking. Sea gulls were flying all around, swooping down to peck at the stuff left near the taco truck by the stacks of lumber. We were happy. We weren't worried. We weren't hurting anyone.

—

Reading in *The New Yorker* about Lincoln's friendship with Stanton— how they would meet at the Soldiers' Home in DC, where peacocks were grounded with blocks tied to their ankles with string. On hot summer days, while talking, Lincoln and Stanton would "untangle peacocks."

—

I rode my bike around the lake yesterday and saw Johnnie running. He must be the last man in Oakland to wear plain gray cotton sweats. Everyone else is all glammed up, even the old men in their polyester sweat suits with the Raiders silver stripes.

He stopped and stared at me, trying to catch his breath.

"You know," he said, "I could just kiss you right now. I should just kiss you."

I was standing behind my bike as if it were a shield. I leaned toward him, involuntarily, and then I pulled back. A mother with a crying baby in a stroller veered around us, frowning because we were blocking the path.

I laughed and said, "I'll see you later," and pedaled away, wobbling until I got up some speed.

———

He'd hate me—wouldn't he?—if I compromised his marriage and his integrity and all he's worked for since he got out of prison and got clean. And I wouldn't like him if he were the kind of man who'd betray his wife.

———

I go to the dentist and she tells me that the crown I got a few years ago was badly done and should be replaced. And I should have a root canal. "I went into debt for that crown," I say. "I'm still paying for it. Can't you just pull that tooth? It's in the back, no one will see it."

Appalled, she explains to me that they never want to pull a tooth. "Every tooth is precious. You could live till you're 95. You need to take the long view." I tell her I'll think about it.

———

Marcus cracked a tooth when he had a nightmare and panic attack last week. His grandmother can't get time off work to take him to the dentist, so I said I'd do it. But first I had to make a lot of calls to get him a replacement Medi-Cal card. When he finally got it, we made a plan to meet at Western Dental downtown. He arrived on his skateboard. We waited a long time and when they finally called him in, he gave me his skateboard to hold. My meter was about to expire so I ran out to put some coins in it. I had no idea how long we'd be at the clinic. In the street, people were smiling at me. Then I realized it was because I was an unlikely person to be walking around with this skateboard. Marcus has painted it with his tag, JOOS.

When I got back to the waiting room there was a father with two little kids and a baby. People came in and out. I was the only white person in the room. Suddenly Marcus appeared in a dental bib. "They want to pull three teeth. Should I let them?"

I went back to talk with the dentist. Aren't teeth precious? Apparently his aren't. Medi-Cal won't pay for repairs. We decided that they should pull just the tooth he broke in his sleep, and another one that is rotten.

I went back to the waiting room. The TV was turned to Jerry Springer. The father with his kids watched me watching TV, trying, I think, to figure out what was up with me and Marcus. Or whether I was trustworthy. He needed to put coins in his meter. He asked me if I could watch his kids for a minute. They were on the floor, playing with Matchbox cars.

"OK," I said, and I sat down to be of use.

—

Since I've resigned myself to the situation with Johnnie, I'm composed, but far from indifferent. It's like I have a built-in sensor. I'm always aware when he's in or around the building. But when I see him now, I keep moving.

One day he stops me in the hall. "You'll see, you'll see—it's not over for us," he says, out of the blue, as if he thinks about us all the time, as if we're having an ongoing conversation. I guess we are, somehow.

"It's not over," he says again, and I don't know what he means, though I'd like that to be true.

But there's nothing I can do. He loves his wife and she loves him, till death do them part. I believe in that.

—

A week later I see him lifting weights. He sees me before I can walk away. He drops the weights and walks toward me.

"You know, I've thought about it and I've prayed on it," he said. "I love you, you know."

I'm shocked to hear him say it. And though it seems ridiculous, I believe him. Because I feel the same way.

He picks the weights up off the floor, and I go downstairs to take my shower.

I always use the open showers, but today I go behind a curtain so I can cry.

—

Last night in Whole Foods I saw Andrew ahead of me in line with a woman. A new girlfriend, I guess. There have been many, including some who heard their biological clock ticking and were sent packing. I watched as he paid for the groceries with his alumni credit card. YALE is printed in such a large font, I could see it from the end of the line. Such a showoff. Does he tell the girls that I was the one who paid off his Yale loans?

Don't be bitter, Linda.

—

Valentine's Day started with an email from Andrew telling me that he is getting married. I'm in shock. He can't have known this woman for more than six months. He tells me they want to do right by Isabel; he's told his fiancée L. that I'm an amazing mother; she's looking forward to co-parenting with me on my terms.

My terms? I want my whole life back. I want a family and a home. I want a new start too.

How old is she? Fourteen years younger than he is. She must want kids? She does. He's willing to have more kids? Since when? How can he afford that? Are they going to keep living in his apartment?

I say, "This will be a shock to Isabel, after she's lived alone with you all these years. Can you get a place where she has her own bathroom and doesn't have to share with you two?"

"Yes," he says. "Anything you want."

"But wait—how can you afford that in Oakland? Rent for a two-bedroom with two baths is impossible on what you make."

He mutters something I can't hear.

"You're not telling me that you're going to buy a house?" He's always wanted a nice house and the kind of lifestyle he expected—his parents' lifestyle—

"Yes," he says, "we're looking at houses."

How is this possible?

He says that his fiancé has been "saving up for a down payment." She's 34, recently moved here from New York City, in school—what kind of work was she doing to save that much money?

I say nasty things I'll regret tomorrow. He doesn't lose his cool. Never loses his cool.

I hang up. I try to sleep. I get up and Google the few things I know about her. Click click click, and I find pictures of her with her parents on one of their trips around the world. She has money.

—

Two days later he tells me that they've watched a lot of Boston movies together so she can learn more about my "culture." "She knows you've had it tough," he says, "and she respects that."

"Fuck you," I say, and I hang up the phone.

I drink half a glass of wine and call him back. He picks up on the first ring.

"Which movies?" I ask.

"Mystic River, The Departed, Gone Baby, Gone."

"Gone, Baby, Gone?"

No no no. This is so wrong.

"Fuck you!"

I hang up again.

An hour later I call him back, crying. "Your life is just beginning and mine is ending. Isabel will leave and I'll be alone and you'll have everything I ever wanted—a family. A real family." And then I sob.

He listens, and when I've exhausted myself he says, "It will be alright" in that deep voice that always made me think he must be right.

The next morning I email him from work.

"How about Scorsese? *Raging Bull* and *Goodfellas*. Tell her that Joe Pesce is going to play my Ma in my biopic."

He emails right back: "Very funny."

I dial his number. He picks up right away.

"Really," he asks, "who would you want to play you in the movie of your life?"

I'm supposed to be played by someone prettier than I am, right? Isn't that how biopics work?

"Marisa Tomei," I say. "But she'll have to gain twenty pounds like De Niro did when he played Jake LaMotta."

—

I think I'm losing my mind. I drive by Andrew's new house. There are Mexicans all over the roof and Salvadorans are mowing the grass, and a guy who looks like Kerouac is tiling a path. It's going to be beautiful, as long as I don't break all the windows.

—

Saw Johnnie on the steps yesterday. I nodded and kept walking.

Anguish. And shame. I wanted to make him love me. I couldn't stop. It took a long time.

And now he does. What have I done?

I'll concentrate on Isabel and work and Marcus. And maybe go away again.

—

To Boston. Visiting with Carlo and Tina and their daughters Ling-Li and Yuan. I hadn't realized that they live on Beaconsfield in Brookline, right near the site of the hotel where my father's mother worked as a domestic up to the end of her pregnancy, hiding her shame. Sometimes I think her shame and my father's shame are the root of mine—a kind of inherited doom, a curdling rage.

I rang the bell at Carlo's. I'd brought chocolate and two Beanie Babies and my new chapbook, *Hesitation Kit*. The girls grabbed everything from me at the door. Yuan, who cannot read yet, immediately sat on the floor with my book, paged through it intently, and yelled triumphantly, "Look! There are words!"

—

Back in Oakland. Sitting at the counter at Lukas, writing furiously in my notebook, oblivious to what's happening around me. Finally the guy to my left just can't stand it anymore.

"Hey," he whispers in my ear, "you seem really absorbed in what you're doing there."

Startled, I look up. "Yes, I am," I say, and I look back down at my notes. But he just starts talking about himself, the way they do.

Picture me dead and buried, and some guy in the grave next door trying to break my concentration . . .

—

Marcus is still on probation and Dick Cheney is still free. Sick country.

Court date is next week. I submitted my report, assuring the judge that Marcus is working toward his GED and should be let off probation and allowed to continue in the foster care system for one more year with subsidy.

Yesterday I learned that I need to provide proof of Marcus's enrollment in an adult school, since he's dropped out of high school. I take a sick day to get it. I go out to East Oakland and wait in a trailer (the office at the adult school) for a clerk to give me the paperwork.

"Take a seat."

I'm the only white person there. People come and go and get their paperwork. The young clerks conspicuously ignore me for a while, comparing their gel nails. I know what I look like to them: a white lady who wants to save black kids and get a prize for it. The whole thing—history, this situation, me being here—it's all fucked up. I know. I'm being tested, and the only way to pass today's test is to shut up and wait and not make it all about me.

Finally one of them calls me up to the counter.

"What can I do for you?" she says.

Almost like a dare.

And everything goes fine from there.

———

At our court date, things go right, despite the fact that Marcus's public defender, an Irish American with the bulbous nose of an alcoholic, calls him the wrong name, again and again, in his statements to the judge. Marcus's other attorney, the one assigned by the dependency courts, is brilliant on his behalf. Marcus will not be locked up. And he'll have a year to get his GED, and the stipend will continue. In the hallway Marcus's grandmother surprises me with a hug before she heads back to tell her prayer group that God heard them.

They say that we can go downstairs to expunge his juvenile criminal record. The door to the clerk's office is locked for her safety. I hit the buzzer a little too hard and wave to her through the glass.

"I have the same bracelet," she says, pointing to my fake ivory jewelry, and we laugh, because we know we got a deal. She makes quick work of our papers.

In the car Marcus says, "Did you see that? She let you right in because you're white."

I said, "Yes, but some black folks are suspicious of all white people, and I can see why."

"Well, not her," he said.

"You're probably right. Maybe my whiteness made it easier to get through that door. Or maybe it was the bracelet. Anyway, today it's making your life better."

I don't tell him about my long afternoon waiting for help at the adult school.

After I dropped him off at his grandmother's I heard an an ice cream truck on 65th Street playing that old standard, "Turkey in the Straw," with a deep rap beat mixed in under the melody.

—

In seven months, I've logged hundreds of hours getting us through the system, writing reports, driving Marcus around and feeding him, spending money I don't have, talking with social workers and attorneys and teachers and the court-mandated (white) psychologist who cautioned me to keep my distance from Marcus as he might be dangerous. I'm tired. But most of all I'm relieved.

The forest fires up north have cast a pall over Oakland. I drive Marcus home in air that's thick and hard to breathe. I drop him off downtown. Now he is—free.

—

I go through my book of Fridays—the journals I kept about our after-noons together and my notes for the reports I wrote for the judge, telling the court what it wanted to hear in language it could understand. Leaving out the most important stuff, the stuff you can't say.

Now I have more time to do what I want to do. What do I want to do?

—

What can I do? My ex-, who has so much, is going to have even more. Two children as soon as possible. That's what his wife wants. While my only child is going to be leaving for college.

I want to smash the state, or someone's face, or patriarchy. Instead I'll go on a date with a guy I met at Di Bartolo's last week while getting coffee. His name is Michael. He comes on too strong for me, and he's not tall, and he has an odd voice with a touch of helium in it. But he's handsome and charismatic and funny. He code-switched twice in the coffee shop, putting on a bit of a show for me as he made small talk with an old woman in a wheelchair and a kid with awesome dreads who was taking out the trash. Of course I interrogated him; is he really single? He has four kids from two marriages. His divorce, he says, will be final soon. He walked me to my car and in the parking lot and he asked me if he could hug me. I said no, not yet. I don't even know the guy.

He's strong as hell. Tight T-shirt. Gorgeous arms. God how I want to be touched.

—

Third date. Time to leap. Drove to his house in El Sobrante. A brand new four-bedroom, two-bath ranch, high up in the hills. How can he afford it? He says the bank was throwing money at him. I look around, skeptical. He lives high off the hog, as my mother would say. He is at work at the auto body shop every morning at six. But still. How does he manage this? The cars and the house, and the kids from two marriages. Is it smoke and mirrors?

He tells me about his childhood. He is the youngest of five. His mother was amazing. A nurse who went back to school for a PhD, a Catholic from New Orleans.

I tell him about my childhood. I'm the oldest of five. My mother was . . . not like his mother.

He has never been back East, "But I know all about Boston." He remembers that Pulitzer Prize-winning picture of white Irish people impaling a Black man with a flagpole the year of the bicentennial.

"Are you from Southie?" he asks.

In other words: Are your people ignorant racists? Did I see them on the news throwing rocks at school buses?

"No. Not quite. I'm from Dorchester."

Same thing.

"Up South," he says, and I tell him about the white neighbor who came to our door in 1970, threatening my father when he put that little house on the market so we could move to the South Shore. "Don't sell to the Colored or else."

He laughs. "Talk in your Boston accent."

"Talk dirty to you? No," I say. "Not now. Some othah time."

I tell him that I never heard anyone in my family say the N word when I was growing up. He says that's impossible. He says that I must have heard it and blocked it out because it would have been too traumatic for me to know that the people I loved hated the people I was going to love.

He lifts me up and puts me on the kitchen counter.

An hour later he jumps out of bed, naked, and grabs two shoeboxes from a shelf. He brings them to the bed and opens them. They're filled with aging portraits and snapshots. He places the pictures on the coverlet as if he's setting up a game of solitaire.

"Oh wow, where'd you get these? From your mother? They're so beautiful!"

"Hey, hey, now," he says. "Let's not start crying. Let's just cuddle and look at pictures of old Negroes."

—

He comes over with a Paul Mooney DVD. After we watch it I make him some night breakfast, bacon and eggs and toast, and we sit on the bed eating and talking. I tell him that, in fact, now I do remember hearing the N word growing up. They used to call the cheapest balcony seats at Boston Garden "n***** heaven."

He laughs. "And I bet no one in your family could even afford those tickets."

—

Last night at dinner he introduced me to his daughter Somaya. Michael was twenty when she was born. He's told us a lot about each other. She's charismatic, funny, and talkative like her father, honest like her mother, and hard-working like both of them.

At dinner when he got up to use the bathroom she whispered to me, "My father says all women are crazy. I tell him, 'Are they really crazy, Dad, or do you make them crazy?'"

"What does he say?" I asked.

"He just laughs, 'cause he knows I'm right."

—

He was speeding on his Ducati on Highway One near Muir Beach last week when a cop pulled him over.

Cop: "Sir, do you know why I pulled you over?"

Michael: "'Cause you're bored and I'm Black?"

I frown, hoping he didn't really say that, hoping that it's a Paul Mooney joke and he's just playing.

I say, "Maybe you can get away with that in Marin on a Ducati. But you wouldn't do that in Oakland, would you? Would you?"

His lack of fear impresses me and scares me. Is he insane?

—

Last week I found a note under my door: Could we please tone it down? Apparently the creaking bed wakes the little boys downstairs. I was mortified, but Michael thought it was hilarious. He high-fived me, proud he'd broken my marriage bed. On Saturday he took it apart and moved it to the cellar. And then we went to Ikea to get a new frame, which he put together in half an hour.

—

He's insane.

The other night he picked me up in his enormous truck. We drove to the Coliseum laughing (he's so entertaining, and he gets my jokes). We were going to see LeBron against the Warriors. But on the way to the game, he cut three people off on 880, laughing like a mad man. As we pulled into the parking lot, the attendant told him it was cash only.

But he didn't have enough cash and he got pissed. He drove through the gate, burning rubber, and the security guard started chasing the truck. Michael high-tailed it out of there, laughing triumphantly while I looked on in shock.

"We're not going to see LeBron?"

Those tickets must have cost $200 each.

He stuck his tongue out at me and threw the tickets out the window.

"Sweetheart, we're going out for steak and milk shakes. I know just the place."

—

The next day he asked for forgiveness so charmingly and so persistently, I gave in.

He loves drama. He also loves make-up sex. I can see why he's twice divorced. And why he'll always be able to get another girlfriend, no matter how he fucks up.

Two days later he picked me up at the gym as Johnnie pulled up in his car.

Johnnie was wearing a suit and fedora. I saw him see us. He lifted his chin, held his head high, and walked right past me.

—

I was having a drink with Michael on Telegraph and ran into Gigi. She was tipsy and in a girlish mood. He's a big flirt, too, so they had fun while she was waiting for her date.

When Michael went to the men's room, she gave me the thumbs up and purred, "I've always wanted a black man." She shook her ass, or what there is of it—she's as slender as a twelve-year-old. She thinks that's why her married boyfriend is into her—his wife is fat. She went off to a table in the back to wait for him.

On the way back to the car I told Michael what she'd said.

"I know her type," he laughed.

"What is her type?" I asked.

He picked me up and swung me around and didn't answer me. Ah yes. It was those strong arms in a tight T-shirt that got me into this.

And now I have to get out. And be alone again.

I came home to an anonymous email warning me about him. His second ex-wife, I think—the white one. But how did she find me? She doesn't need to warn me. I'm onto him. I'm done.

2009

Some of Those Stars

Oscar Grant, unarmed, on his belly, shot in the back and killed by police at Fruitvale Station. Caught on video. How many times has this happened in American history and there was no evidence? And even when there is evidence, like that video of Rodney King, the police are unaccountable.

At work in a team meeting, small talk turns to things in the news—a Black president! I mention Oscar Grant. My boss shakes his head. "If he'd just stayed down and done what the police told him to do, he'd still be alive."

No one says anything. Ben and I exchange glances. Jennifer tilts her head and smiles brightly at I don't know what.

I'm the oldest on our team. They can make my life miserable but they can't fire me. I should speak.

"But he did stay down. He was as down as he could be when they shot him."

They ignore me. But I'm sure they heard me.

—

And Marcus—where is Marcus? He has disappeared. His grandmother says she hasn't seen him since he got off probation.

—

White anarchists come to Oakland to smash windows and set things on fire and then they go home to Berkeley. The cop who shot Oscar Grant lives in Napa. Why don't they go to Napa and tear it up? Or to Marin? Or down to Fourth Street in Berkeley, where the ice cream costs six dollars a scoop. Are there no racists in those places? Nothing that needs to be smashed or broken or lit up?

The phone rings, a number I don't recognize.

"Hey."

It's Marcus calling from a new phone.

"My grandmother said you'd be thinking of me. She said I should call you."

"I'm glad you did."

We make a plan to meet at Lanesplitter.

—

Inauguration night. Isabel and I go to Jack London Square for a block party near Everett and Jones. We're the only white people there. We stand on the curb at the back of the crowd while people dance in the street. On a huge outdoor movie screen, they're repeating a holy trinity of images: a lynching in the Jim Crow South; the face of the first Black president; and a picture of Oscar Grant. I explain to Isabel, as succinctly as possible, why these things go together.

I grew up kneeling beneath Jesus on the cross. It doesn't seem strange to me that suffering and crucifixion and resurrection are part of the same story.

—

Bells in the campanile played "Lift Every Voice and Sing" tonight as I was leaving work.

In the locker room the tune comes into my head and I start to hum as I put my clothes on. In the other rows, a few women start to hum along. Then we sing the words softly.

As I leave, I look down the aisles and note that each of the singers is white. Someone apparently taught us something.

—

Stanley calls to tell me that he and Susan took the F train all the way into Manhattan to see *La Bohème*. It was a long trip but they were exhilarated. I'm sure she was dressed to the nines. He was so excited on the phone, he started sing-humming.

Then Richard called and we got to remembering the Clancy Brothers concert in Southie and he started to sing–shout "Haul Away Joe" and I sang along.

Isabel listened and laughed while she did her homework.

—

Last night Isabel explained that a violin piece was difficult because she didn't even know there was a note like G natural.

Tonight her practice was beautiful and deliberate and sour. Sounded like she was squeezing juice from citrus fruits.

Walter Benjamin: I would like to make something from books the way wine is made from grapes.

—

Tulsa and Rosewood—the few white families who offered shelter to Black people—very few—

The same stars that looked down on the crucifixion—some of those stars presided over lynchings—and look down on us now—

—

Without Sin

Pale green carnations
Mint and lime
Clean incense and a linen remnant
Appealing to no conscience
Sacramental
In a blood-red light.

We always heard
It would be white
But it's not white

—

"Every woman who has ever kept a diary knows that women write in diaries because things are not going right." – From Mary Helen Washington's introduction to the Memphis diaries of Ida B. Wells

—

The perfect book, one in which I write between the lines.

—

Have not seen Johnnie for a long while. There's a new mayoral administration. Maybe Johnnie lost his job and is back to working in East Oakland or Hayward with guys in the halfway house, teaching anger management and going to a gym down there?

—

Even the most incorrigible maverick has to be born somewhere. [She] may leave the group that produced [her]—[she] may be forced to—but nothing will efface [her] origins, the marks of which [she] carries with her everywhere. I think it is important to know this and even find it a matter for rejoicing, as the strongest people do, regardless of their station. On this acceptance, literally, the life of a writer depends. – James Baldwin, from "The Discovery of What It Means to Be an American"

(And of course the writer must constantly change the pronouns to include herself in all that she reads—"rejoicing, even" that she has lived long enough to learn to do this.)

2010

If the Fool Would Persist

Last night I went to Seder at Naomi's. She asked me to bring dessert. Her Chanukah parties and Seders and her kids' bar mitzvahs are highlights of my spiritual life. Every year at these gathering someone asks me if I'm Jewish and Naomi tells them that I'm Jew-ey. Mindlessly this year I made bread pudding for her Seder. I'll never live this down.

—

Two weeks ago June invited me to a fancy fundraiser for children of incarcerated parents, and there I met a lawyer named William who does policy work to disrupt the school-to-prison pipeline. We struck up a conversation, talked about the system, and decided to get together later. When I got home I Googled him and learned that he's really good at what he does. But in the pictures online he looks merely overweight. In person he is morbidly obese.

Last night I met him for dinner at Le Cheval. We put our napkins in our laps. His covered only a tiny portion of his enormous belly and thighs, like a loin cloth.

I said, "Did you always know that you were supposed to put the napkin in your lap? 'Cause I didn't learn it until I went to college. We put our napkins under our chins like bibs."

He said his mother had taught him etiquette and such. He said his parents were very involved in the NAACP when his father was stationed in Norfolk, and they met a white family named Dineen who was also involved in the struggle. The Dineens invited his family to dinner.

I said, "Oh, Dineen is my sister-in-law's maiden name. Her father was a New York City police detective."

The NYPD, a kind of anti-NAACP.

William looked at me as if I were a subordinate who'd interrupted his monologue.

"Go on," I said.

"We had never been invited to white folks' house. My mother made us practice our table manners over and over before the big night. But when we got there we found out that the Dineens were slobs. They didn't care about nothing but The Cause. There were pamphlets and posters and papers piled all over every surface. Mrs. Dineen stirred the gravy with her cigarette hanging out of her mouth, the ash about to fall into the pan any minute. When we sat down to eat she just shoved all the paperwork onto the floor. They didn't have no napkins and their plates were chipped and didn't match. Those white folks were like John Brown or something. Fanatics!"

"What a great story," I said. But he didn't seem to understand why it was funny, or why it might appeal to me.

"Hmmmp," he said. "I don't care much for stories."

Suddenly I remembered learning about the four humors, sanguine, bilious, phlegmatic, and melancholic. Here was an example of the phlegmatic.

He seemed fatter than he was when I met him two weeks ago. It's like he has a two-foot barrier all around him, and in this way he reminded me of someone unlike him in most respects: my mother.

He has never married or lived with a woman, but he says he plans to look for a companion when he retires.

I said, "Do you think it will be that easy to find someone whenever you're ready?"

He snorted and said, "I'm a black man with a job. There'll always be some black woman who'll put up with me."

Hmmm.

I asked him about his family. He said his mother and sister had both died in the last few years. He'd helped with some insurance paperwork but had been on the road, giving keynote speeches and so on, and had been too busy to be there when they passed. I murmured condolences but he brushed them off; he wasn't sad. I asked him if he had children. He hesitated and said yes. A white woman in law school had wanted to have a child and raise it on her own. He'd already scheduled a vasectomy but agreed to inseminate her by appointment.

He seems to take a purely administrative approach to all human affairs.

He doesn't like kids, really. Doesn't have the patience. He said he admires me for my work in the foster care system, though his sister, a social worker, doesn't believe in white people raising Black kids, "but someone's gotta do it."

"I'm not raising them," I said. "I'm an adjunct. And I understand your sister's point of view."

(I didn't bother to add: When we were teenagers, Ma used to call the Department of Child Services and scream and beg them to take us off her hands. Adolescents of any race are not in high demand.)

Next we talked about non-profit accounting and houseplants. He's researching the purchase of a large rubber plant for his foyer. He talked about that for a long time. When I tried to break up his monologue, he leaned back with his hands over his belly, waited for me to shut up, and picked up where he'd left off.

—

Why do I waste my time on men? I give up. I'll just have to marry myself. Carry myself over the threshold into the next phase of my life.

—

Home from the Russian River with Isabel. On the beach in our secluded spot she lounged in her bikini reading *Lolita*. I asked her what she thought of the book. "It's beautifully disgusting."

—

"If the fool would persist in [her] folly, [she] would become wise." – William Blake

I certainly have persisted.

Looking through thirty years of notebooks—stitching, remembering, juxtaposing. Imposing order that isn't there while you're living it.

Poet's Work

Grandfather
advised me:
Learn a trade

I learned
to sit at desk
and condense

No layoff
from this
condensery

    —Lorine Niedecker

     —

I thought "work" was: doing everything they told you to do, or anticipating their needs. I was a hard worker.

     —

I have been light-headed with fear about the birth of Isabel's brother—Oliver—the start of Andrew's new family. I was afraid I'd break down as soon as I saw him. But that didn't happen.

Andrew put him on the bed and I leaned over him, marveling. Andrew sat on the other side of him. For a moment it was as if we were looking at our baby again, and we were happy.

Isabel will be OK with it if I am OK, right? So I try to be OK. And how can I not fall in love with the baby?

The glorification of whiteness is everywhere, including language—"He has fine hair." "She is fair." "He is dark."—"Her coarse hair." How to speak or write or live without complicity?

The new baby is blue-eyed and so blond. Andrew has become more and more white since we split up, and his new marriage amplifies that privilege exponentially. And I have become more and more—what?

—

Publishing a book—*The Public Gardens*—half poetry, half prose—

What if no one reads it?

What if someone reads it?

What will I right next?

I mean, what will I write next?

—

Marcus asked, "Am I in your book?"

"No," I said. "It's about a time before I knew you. But you can be on my book." And so he is, in a way. I pulled out that old black-and-white photo of a stranger and made a collage for the cover, and that young man stands in for Marcus. And for Johnnie and Billy Strayhorn and James Baldwin and my brother, and others. And their mothers.

—

I'm packing up to move a few blocks away to a nicer, more expensive rental. Marcus came over to help us decorate the tree and we ate pizza among the boxes. He has never been to my place before. It wasn't allowed when he was a minor and I was representing him in court. But now we are out of the system, making it up as we go along.

—

I was alone in my apartment on Christmas afternoon while Isabel spent the holiday with her father's new family. It rained hard. I binged on "Mad Men" and wine, surrounded by moving boxes.

I checked my email and found a message from a Stanford professor, MK's husband, a translator of Celan. He had a publishing question. I wrote back right away, thrilled at the excuse to ignore this Christian holiday that seems designed to punish me and so many other strays.

Then Stanley called. He always calls me on Christmas, Valentine's Day, and Easter.

Abruptly he said, "You are not married again yet?"

What? I'd seen him and Susan twice in the spring and he was up to date on everything important in my life, or everything that I could bear to tell him.

"What did you say?"

"Are you married? Have you remarried yet?"

He sounded annoyed with me, or disappointed. Was he losing his mind? He'd always been so kind.

"No," I said, feeling like a failure. "I'm still all alone."

—

Waiting for Isabel to come back from Andrew's, I went down to the cellar to sort my junk. My marriage bed was there in pieces. I pulled all the pieces up to the sidewalk. Then I went upstairs to my desk and posted something on the free-cycle section of Craigslist and waited at the window. Eight minutes later a young white couple with dreads pulled up in a truck to take it all away.

And that was the end of that.

Translations for an Imaginary Audience

Gather up the fragments that remain, that nothing be lost.

Gospel of John

Book of

my heart   moveth out of place

the noise of his voice   his mouth   whole heaven

when his voice is heard   beasts go cold

great things do he   to the snow

likewise to the small rain

stand still and consider   garments warm   quiet earth

spread out the sky   a looking glass

be swallowed up

From The Book of Job

Found

Of course he wasn't dead.
He could never be dead until she herself
had finished feeling and thinking.
                                    Zora Neale Hurston

Your sweet loving
dark and beautiful
black lily
in a field
of thistles

Your flag is love
your left hand
beneath my head
your right arm
holding me close

My beloved
and my friend
much sweeter
than all other
pleasures

I could not find you,
I called your name—
Love
fierce as
death

The curve of your cheek
in the garden—
your plot
across from a sign—
Devotion

Wherever we lie
our bed is green
I lie down on you
a feast in a field
of black lilies

After the Song of Songs

Stain

Salada, Lipton, Red Rose
dregs stain the paper
the color of the Wampanoag
the parchment in the museum
where you learned a little about Indians.

Wessagusset, now that's a beautiful word.
The first printing of a Bible
in the colonies was a translation
into Massachuset.
Who now reads Massachuset?

We were sunning at Nantasket
after Mass in Scituate
and a lunch of iced tea and sandwiches.
We stretched out on the jetty.
and put clamshells over our eyelids.
I have a Polaroid of us
smiling. Brown.
White bassinet
in the foreground.

Dream After Reading Pasternak

Last night I dreamed that Wanda called me about community college, but her name was Lara.

Lara's favorite color was mauve of lilac in bud. She liked to sit in the violet dusk at the shop near the black-current caramels in glass jars.

Wanda goes to junior college near the birthplace of the Black Panthers, on the other side of the lake. I can almost see it from my window looking toward the Port of Oakland.

In my dream when my mother saw Wanda, she said what she always used to say. The reason I ran away.

Then my mother died, and Wanda was "transbluent," neither Union nor Confederate, neither Black nor Greek. At the wake, I wore mauve toenail polish, a shade called "Call Your Mother."

"Next year in Jerusalem," whispered Tip O'Neill. He was davening on the steps to the polls, counting precincts. Catholics don't daven and this is not the kind of thing he'd say, but I heard it anyway.

•

When we were little we lived near the house where Malcolm X had lived. He stayed there with his sister when he first came to Boston. I didn't know this when I was a girl. On my desk I have a picture of his old house, a woman standing on the front porch, staring suspiciously at the camera.

•

In the refugee camps in Jordan where it was crowded and dry, Jean Genet would look up at the sky: "Clouds are nutritious." In Palestine he thought of Oakland and the Panthers, souls shipwrecked by the Church, prisons and pietas. Prisons he found rather motherly.

•

Mourning for Lara, Zhivago also mourned that distant summer when the revolution had come down to earth from heaven. Grieving, he looked at bruise-colored clouds and thought of politics.

"All politics is local," said Tip O'Neill. Except for mystics.

My Little Brown Book

Gathered here today, a one-woman congregation with passwords to *The Encyclopedia of Human Emotions, The Encyclopedia of Rose Science, The Encyclopedia of Ham,* and a history of noise.

Micro-, Macro-, and Propaedia, concordances of feathers and petals, bricks and high dimples of recorded sound, the scream of anti-melody.

Archives of the funny papers and a definition of "rose blindness," and "The ham, v. much divorced from the pig." An index of questions beginning and ending with infants.

iTunes starts shuffling: James Brown under something too low to get under, and then music in a minor key, an elemental brown, soundtrack to a database of the slave trade.

In the digital archives of *The Boston Globe,* I search the parishes of my childhood and find reports about adjacent neighborhoods. They burned her house down. They killed his son. Rats crawled across the crib. Reporters went to the ghetto and wrote stories with adverbs: "She smiled sadly." "He laughed wearily." Bad translations for an imaginary audience. No one ever did anything angrily, at least in the liberal paper. Except for the time they torched that poor girl. No adverbs needed.

How to bear it without wine and music? I run down to the Quikstop near the lake. "Brown Sugar" stockings on a rack near the locked-up liquor and four-packs of ibuprofen. Emergency supplies of "ultra, ultra-sheer" pantyhose.

A little girl sits on the box behind the register next to her mother. Girls and their mothers always make me want to write.

(Angrily)

(Putting away the case)

(Finds a piece of paper and starts to draw large letters on it)

(Laughing herself)

(Regarding them for a long time as they dance)

(Goes to door and opens it)

(Smoothing her hair with slight embarrassment)

(Drily)

(With appreciation of the two meanings)

(With a grand and bitter gesture)

(She is smiling, teasingly)

(Her arms folded saucily)

(Giggling fiercely)

(From her room)

(Plaintively)

Experience

On your bicycle, skateboard, or motorcycle / Or in that wreck of a car that makes poor people pity me / Or at the bakery with hairnets and German chocolate cupcakes / Where we met Ebony / who fell in love with her mother in a hot tub / And that time in the paternity ward / In a gingham shirt I never saw again / Where you laughed when I insulted a nun / Because of something she'd never done

You, harangued by a beauty on the phone / You, suffering in a shower stall / It is safer in a meat locker / Or at that wall near Marcus Books / Another wall you improved / "Emancipated from care"

With for or against / People need to listen / People need to speak / Or dress up like the police / Impersonating order / Blowing things up on Independence Day and burning your hand / "What to the slave is the Fourth of July?"

This balm is made of Vaseline / This one you made of spit and samples / From the paint store where you used to work / Black white and a little blue / Makes a color you call JOOS

Lyric Episodes: Journals

2011

Di Maise Iz Ois

Corey called to tell me that Stanley had died. When I called her back she said, "I just kept saying to everyone, 'Who will call Linda? We have to tell Linda.'"

"How is Susan?"

"She's a wreck, as you can imagine. I don't know how long she'll last without him. But I wonder if you know, Linda, that you made my father-in-law so happy. He kept your letters on the table in the hall. The one with the sprigs of jasmine in the envelope—he held it up to my nose once."

Stanley—my friend for almost twenty-five years. Forty-five years older—more like a father to me than my own father ever was—

My God—he must have known he was dying when he called me at Christmas—he was worried about leaving me alone in this world—that's why he asked me about being married—

Di maise iz ois. The story is over.

—

Marcus's 21st birthday. I make dinner and a cake for him. He brings Rachel, his on-and-off-again girlfriend. She is home from college in New England. I wish he would go to college. That's what his grandmother wants, too. Maybe Laney, maybe next semester.

Isabel listens and says little. Sometimes she's like this and then later, when we're alone, she talks a blue streak. She is just getting to know Marcus. And how does he feel about all of this? A direct question may get me nowhere. I'll have to wait and see. And listen.

—

He calls me a few days later. He and Rachel had a big fight. He threw a couch at her—that huge couch he found on the street and carried on his back for twenty blocks when he first moved into that apartment with Harrell. I hope his anger doesn't kill him or anyone else.

Plenty of times when I would have thrown a couch if I'd been strong enough.

"I've thrown a lot of stuff," I tell him. "Salt. Dishes. Magazines." Pause. "My friend the professor once threw lentils at her husband."

He laughs.

"And once," I say, "I poured a cup of milk on my mother's head so she'd stop hitting my brother."

It seemed the most non-violent option at the time.

"What happened next?"

She slammed the door on my hand and broke my finger and kept screaming though I begged her to stop. Then she kicked me out and I had to sleep at the Falzones' house. That was the week I was supposed to be studying for the SATs.

I answer Marcus. "I don't remember."

Then I suggest some ways to maybe not throw couches. Techniques. And I think of Johnnie, who would know how to help.

—

Amazing email today about my book from Phillip Lopate, a writer I've admired for so long. Can this really be happening to me? Have I redeemed myself?

—

One day after Isabel was born, I was up in Boston, poking around in my mother's hope chest, looking for old report cards, and I found my I.Q. test. One hundred and forty-four. A genius. Of course, those tests don't matter, are biased, all that. But still.

"Hey, Ma. Why didn't you ever tell me I was kind of a genius?"

"I didn't want you to get no ideas. Didn't want you to get conceited."

*In the hope chest I also found my cedar-scented acceptance letter for
Girls Latin. I was so proud of that then. But the letter was signed by
Louise Day Hicks, the racist who was head of the school board. And I
never ended up going to Latin, because my parents, like so many other
white people in Boston in 1970, moved across the city line to escape
"forced busing" and "racial strife."*

*That was the year a white man showed up at our door in Dorchester and
threatened to kill my father if he sold the house to "the Colored." I re-
member how scared my father was after that encounter, and how drunk
he got. In those days, on his way home from the bus stop every night, he
picked up either a gallon of milk for us or case of beer for himself, carry-
ing the case on his head like an African in* National Geographic.

———

In New York in November for book party and reading at PPOW gallery.
I say, "It's All Saints day." Eileen corrects me. "No, it's All Souls."

Coming out of the Met, walking down Fifth, I hear one brother say to
another: "I mean, this chick was so much fun, I forgot to fuck her. That's
what I want in a woman—that kind of fun."

I went down to Occupy today. I watched the police watching the dem-
onstrators. One little cop who could have been my Sicilian cousin was
wearing a regulation sweater vest over his regulation shirt. He looked like
his mother had dressed him for a school photo. I smiled and said, "I like
your vest." He looked away.

They have everything they need at Zuccotti Park, including a library with
an anarchist-poet-librarian who knows Kevin and Dodie. I promised to
come down again tomorrow, to bring my book to add to the shelves.

———

At the PS1 9/11 anniversary exhibit—walking around, taking notes about the exhibit—

Approximately 200 people jumped or fell, most from the North Tower, 101-107 floors—first building hit, second to fall—none of them conclusively identified. Music to make your face fall off: Cardiff, forty black audio speakers, Tallis motet for 40 voices.

Sign in PS stairway: SEPTEMBER 11 CONTINUES, with an arrow pointing you in the right direction.

—

In Boston for book business. I ask Richard to take me to the airport. It ends up being the opposite of a favor; we have to go drop the cab off with Victor, the guy who owns the medallion. Then Victor will take me to the airport, charging me full price, and I'll have to tip him well, hoping he'll be merciful to my brother.

I take Richard out to breakfast before we drive to Victor's place in Watertown, and I give him fifty dollars. I'm in town to give a reading at Harvard, a most unlikely development. To paraphrase Langston Hughes: our neighborhood in Dorchester was as far from Harvard as Morningside Heights is from Harlem—a stones-throw across an abyss.

Richard hasn't read my book. He's in it, though—all of my brothers are in my book—especially our dead brother, also a writer—so I feel the urge to give though I'm not making any money from the book.

He shouts "Authorette! Authorette!" and laughs maniacally.

But never mind my book. "It's easy to write a book!" he says. He's gonna write his own. "It's a done deal. It's all written in my head. Just get me a contract! I'll give you a cut."

"I'll see what I can do."

—

I ask him to drive me into Mount Auburn Cemetery, one of my favorite places. The poet Robert Creeley is buried here, and Fanny will be. We were both excited for a minute when she bought the plot. Fanny said, "I can hardly wait!" Mount Auburn is glorious in October, when it smells like chestnuts and dusty leaves and books and apples.

On the way to Victor's place, Richard says, "Linda, when Victor gets in the cab, don't say nothin'."

"What do you mean?"

"I mean, just don't say nothin'."

"What? Me? You and Ma and Caroline are always complaining about how quiet I am—how I keep everything to myself. 'Linda don't say nothin'.' I'm the quietest one in this family!"

"Well," he says, "it's true you are quiet. But sometimes you say outrageous things in a quiet way. So just don't say nothin'."

———

He also has a gig driving blind children to and from their special school. It seems to be his only sure thing as far as income goes. Many of them live in the projects. Our aunts used to live in the projects when we were kids, and we were always over there. But then all the white people moved out.

Richard has a soft spot for one of the blind girls, his passenger Bronte. Her father is too disabled to come out to get his beautiful daughter at the curb. My brother walks her right to the door. The father thanks him a hundred times and offers Richard rice and beans with goat meat. But Richard can't leave the cab alone there for long.

Sometimes he picks up black people at night and takes them right into the projects. They call him a crazy white man.

He's enormous now, a bear, bald since he was in his twenties, with blue eyes and wisps of dark hair. He was a beautiful boy and the nurses at the epilepsy clinic loved him, though Sr. Jean and the other nuns did not; he was too strange to be obedient in class, and a little too good to deserve a beating.

In high school he carried a copy of Pascal and wore his pants pulled up too high. There was no escaping my brothers and sister at school. Four of us, so close in age, trying to ignore each other in public. When I'd see Richard in the hallway, I'd turn away.

—

They had a birthday party for him at the blind school when he turned 50 two years ago. One of the girls asked him if she could touch his face. He told me she put her arms around his waist to see how fat he was, and smoothed his head, laughing because he was bald—"I never knew that!" she said. Then she gave him a loud, sloppy kiss that made all the other blind kids laugh.

He's always broke. People cheat him, or he buys too much stuff, I don't know. In high school when he worked at the pizza place he'd forget to cash his checks. My sister and I would find them shredded in his pockets while doing his laundry.

—

Back from the East Coast, feeling good about myself, I see Johnnie downstairs in the gym and I feel poised enough to engage. So I sit on the bench, waiting for him to get off his phone. I miss that voice that made me want to be a better person. He's in a suit, he must have given a talk somewhere today. He's wearing a wedding ring. He wasn't wearing one when I fell in love with him.

He ends his call and turns toward me. People pass between us on their way in and out of the locker rooms. All the women smile at me. All the men acknowledge him.

He's lost weight. Maybe he's sick? He looks at me with such vulnerability that I think my heart will break. I just smile as if I'm fine, as if I've got it together. And I kinda do. But I'm more single than ever. And he's still married.

As I stand up to walk into the locker room, I look back over my shoulder and wave.

"See you."

"Will you?" he says, his voice breaking. He puts his hat over his heart.

"Sure," I said, walking away. "I'll see you around."

My friend Maggie passes me in the hallway, takes it all in, and raises her eyebrows knowingly at this little drama.

I turn the corner knowing he's watching me.

At the sinks, after I've changed into my gym clothes, I run into Maggie again. She's already naked from the waist down. "I saw that," she says. "No one got nothin' on you, girl!" She smiles and gives me the thumbs-up, like I'm a real mankiller.

I start to cry.

She puts her arm around me. "Oh, baby."

—

Reading Eileen's *Inferno*.

"'I want each of you to write an Inferno,'" The teacher says. "The class groaned."

"'It's just this time. This is yours.' She smiled."

"It was ours now," Eileen says. "I would show her my hell."

—

Easter Sunday. Waiting for a call from Stanley that will not come. Easter was a horrible time in Częstochowa, Stanley said. Pilgrims visited the Black Madonna and every year, after the Passion play, there were pogroms.

If he could survive Auschwitz, why can't he survive death and give me a call?

I cried on the phone with Susan last week. We are still in shock, though he was 92.

"Leenda," she said, "You know Stanley didn't even *beeleeve* in death!"

—

Drafts of "Stain" and "Street" taped into my notebooks—the way I used to write poems—

Reading Nella Larsen's *Quicksand*—interesting how she almost parodies Stein's *Melanctha* in the novel *Quicksand*—calling her main character by her full name often and oddly—"Helga Crane"—

"Her own lack of family disconcerted them. No family. That was the crux of the matter."

Helga rebels—remembers a black girl in an orange dress—"Why, she wondered, didn't someone write 'A Plea for Color'?"

"The pink, white, and gold people"

And: "[Anne] hated white people with a deep and burning hatred, with the kind of hatred which, finding itself in sufficiently numerous groups, was capable someday, on some great provocation, of bursting into dangerously malignant fumes."

—

Writing and thinking. It has been years since I saw—oh, so many people. If I had known that leaving my marriage would lead to a cascade of confusion and loss, would I have done it anyway? Yes—because I was so angry. And because leaving that marriage was the only way I could be a good mother.

Sometimes it's hard to sleep, thinking about what I've done and what's been done to me. Me me me. And I think about people I've loved, and other people I don't even know. Night thoughts.

I don't have a will of steel. I get up and have a glass of wine and go back to bed. But I can't sleep, so I get up to eat some bread and cheese in the dark. I drink more wine and, against my better judgment, I turn on the computer to browse the Internet and look up people who disappeared from my life long ago. Then I try to go to sleep.

—

Leah came to me in a dream. As she approached the hospital, the bells tolled. Sometimes the bells stalled. She said: That's because sometimes figuration stalls.

In the dream, Jackie Robinson sailed past in a Mercedes and they nodded at each other. I thought she was going to give me her bib, but she pulled away and said, 'It's not actually for sale. It's a multiple, it not for giving. So I couldn't afford it.

She told me about her children, her marriage, her three lovers, her dealer and her world travels. The life of an art-world insider.

Still dreaming, I sat up and wrote it down.

The next night I saw, beside my bed, what I'd written in my sleep: nothing.

I put down my book and took off my glasses so I could hear better. Two takes of "Solitude," and that piano trill that always stops me in my tracks. Loneliness as honky-tonk, or vice-versa.

2012

Little Miracle

Bob took me out to lunch to celebrate the book. Asked me if I was surprised it had done so well.

"Sure, I'm shocked. I had no expectations. But what really amazes me is that I haven't been *punished* for publishing it."

He laughed. He's Catholic, he knows.

"I never thought anyone would read it. It makes me less lonely, makes other people less lonely."

"A book is a little miracle, isn't it?"

—

The Soul Must Stay Where It Is

> *Do those towers even exist?*
> *We must look at it that way, along those lines*
> *so the thought can erect itself, like plywood battlements.*

John Ashbery, from "A Poem of Unrest"

Friday night in New York, on my way to see Ashbery at Poet's House . . .

As we hurried toward the subway, walking past the hospital where she was born, Isabel offered to come to the reading with me, and I said, "No, no, you go," and I watched her walk down the stairs to the L train to Williamsburg, where she was conceived.

At rush hour I walk toward the Towers, or where the Towers were when I was pregnant seventeen years ago at this time of year in this chartreuse light and heat. When I was married, when I lived in New York, when—when—when—when—

Then.

Go. Go. Go.

Walt Whitman's words from "Crossing Brooklyn Ferry" scroll digitally across the front of an office building. I stop to read and look. Not one of the thousands rushing to New Jersey Transit seems to notice the enormous words:

> *The impalpable sustenance of me from all things at all hours of the day,*
> *The simple, compact, well-join'd scheme, myself disintegrated,*
> *everyone disintegrated yet part of the scheme*

(Would he write a different poem now—about America—)

I stop at Pret a Manger near City Hall to get a sandwich. I'm the only one in the place. I forgot to bring a book. I don't even have a pen. There's nothing to do but look.

I sit still long enough to notice two detectives on the corner. They're well-groomed and camouflaged in suits, still and watchful in the midst of the river of commuters. Hot.

Everyone except me is racing for a train or a cab or the ferry to New Jersey. Thousands of people are passing and the detectives are watching all of them while I watch the detectives.

It's a straight shot to City Hall from here. I can see the limousine pulling out under trees as green as salad, cop cars and police all around. The Mayor will not be killed tonight as he heads out to the Hamptons for the weekend. A phalanx. A word you'd never use unless it's the right one.

I watch the white plainclothes cop next to the black SUV parked illegally. He looks like me: stocky, thick eyebrows, dark. Kind of like the enemy.

"Where are you from?" the old man asked me on the subway platform to Jackson Heights the other day. "Do you speak Arabic?" The next day a lady asked me if I was Iranian. "No," I said, "it's just the Clairol talking." I am still dark, but fading with age.

The white detective has heavy ear lobes. Nice pants. A wedding ring. A boxer's nose.

I'm in awe of his concentration. He sees everything but me. Unwatched, I eat like a pig.

I've been watching the white plainclothes cop for about fifteen minutes. I should go. My hands smell like mayonnaise. I fix my lipstick and walk out onto the sidewalk, hit by a blast of heat and swampy salt air. Two thousand people have passed this cop without seeing him. I make a point of smiling at him as I pass. He doesn't smile back, but I see him flinch at being seen.

At the corner, there's a halal food cart next to trashcans and scaffolding. The proprietor is prostrated on the filthy sidewalk behind his cart, angled toward Mecca (toward Queens). A broker in a suit almost steps on him. A nearly naked anorexic jogger kicks him by accident while waiting for the light to turn. Nothing moves him. Maybe he is also a detective?

I walk toward the water, toward a man with extension cords wrapped around his waist, looking for someplace to be plugged in.

—

Reading library books about gardens:

Morning glory seeds: If the soil is too rich you will get more foliage than flower

They are hard-shelled, they benefit from soaking or scarification

—

I've been thinking about my parents' childhoods since I was a child, trying to figure out how they turned out the way they did. Do they ever think about my childhood?

At her audition for the part of Tony Soprano's mother, Nancy Marchand said to David Chase about Livia (based on his own horrific Italian mother): "I trust the model for this character is deceased?"

Ma told me and Joey, "Don't write about me until I'm dead." But is she dead if she has refused to see me or Isabel these last ten years, despite my attempts to reconnect?

If you lick your wounds and find yourself distracted by the sweet and salty taste, and you reach for a pen to note this, you're a writer.

———

I was proud not to wet my bed when the others were all wetting theirs. The stink—Ma shrieking—everyone cowering—Ma out there in the yard in winter, wrestling with the frozen sheets on the line, whacking them with a baseball bat, the ice shattering on her head.

Ice like the Lucite heels of her tiny wedding shoes, the shoes she kept in a box in the closet with dresses from when she had a waistline. Items I visited occasionally as if on a pilgrimage to a shrine.

———

The college counselor at Isabel's school, Matteo, asked us to come in to start the process, so Andrew and I met in Matteo's yesterday. "First off, what should I know about your family?"

I wait to see if Andrew will say anything about his wife and little kids, but he just smiles at me, so I speak first.

"Well," I said, "I guess you should know that Isabel's father and I are from very different backgrounds."

We each tell him a little about our education—my nuns and Jesuits, his Bennington and Yale. I mention that Andrew speaks Italian; he learned it when he was in high school, living with his family at the American Academy in Rome. I mention that both of his parents were Fulbrights.

Matteo starts to ask another question on his checklist but Andrew interrupts.

"You should probably know that Linda is usually the smartest person in the room, though she's never seemed to understand that. And she just published a critically-acclaimed book."

Did he really just say that?

"That's nice," says Matteo, and then he asks us about parameters— Grades and SATs, scholarships and financial aid, East Coast colleges, Catholic or small or large schools, and UCs—

"No Catholic colleges," I say. Matteo nods and smiles and scribbles a note to himself. He went to an all-boys Catholic high school in LA and he's gay.

In the parking lot when I say goodbye to Andrew I'm brusque. The sky is overcast. I'm cold. And I don't want to cry.

When I get home there's an email from the *Los Angeles Times*. My book is a finalist for their book prize. I'm not allowed to tell anyone. Of course, I call Andrew right away.

—

> *Now in one year*
>   *a book published*
>   *and plumbing—*
>
> *took a lifetime*
>   *to weep*
>   *a deep*
>   *trickle*

(Lorine again . . .)

—

The book festival put us up at the Biltmore for one night. I gave a reading. So did Rodney King. In the VIP room, Judy Blume said hi to me.

I sat under a tent and signed books. The line was long. One guy had already read it. He waited in line to tell me that he loved it. "My favorite part is when Isabel asks you about goodness." All kinds of people like that part—not just Catholics.

Two women were next in line. They beamed at me. "Don't you remember us? We're your cousins!" Kathy and Jennifer, who were so young when I last saw them—what were they doing here? They live in Long Beach. Jennifer stayed after her father was transferred by the airline where he worked, and then Kathy came out to be a baggage handler for American. They'd read my name in the paper and decided to surprise me by showing up. I had no idea any of my 74 cousins lived in California. Our family's so huge, there's actually a flock of exiles and black sheep.

I cancelled my plans for the night and invited them up for room service at my expense. The four of us stretched out on the bed and they told Isabel about that distant world, our world. They reassured me that no one believes the awful things my parents say about me, and we cried.

A lot of great things have happened to me because Pressed Wafer published my book. But this reunion is the best thing by far.

———

Just finished reading Susan Faludi's moving and devastating profile of Shulamith Firestone. Remembering that era of feminism in which I came of age in my own Catholic way—Dworkin and McKinnon and Shange and Lorde, and the time Vee and I and the rest of our little cadre drove to Brown for a feminist conference and, when we showed up for the panel about race, found that the white organizers felt they couldn't have an open discussion with a black woman in the room.

Vee got up and, timidly, we got up, too, and we all walked out, too nice and too intimidated to know what to say to these sophisticated feminists. We wandered around Providence as far as Hope Street. And then we poked around the racks at the vintage store while Bowie's "Heroes" poured from the speakers. Vee and I went back to our room in the garret at the womyn's house. We slept in the same bed. In the dark I could feel her shaking, crying. She reached for my hand.

—

All of Shulamith Firestone's paintings were tossed in the trash when she was evicted near the end of her life. I dream of finding one of them in a Goodwill on Long Island the way I fantasize about finding Strayhorn's original (Oedipal) lyrics to "Satin Doll." Johnny Mercer was called in to write something more appropriate, and Strayhorn's lyrics were lost or destroyed.

—

Taking a six-week meditation class with twenty other people in an upstairs corner room in a Julia Morgan building. Friday afternoons for three hours. It gets dark early and it's awfully cold in there. We spread out on mats with woolen blankets that smell like sheep. I want to cultivate equanimity. But all I do is cry. It's almost Christmas. Those children slaughtered in their classroom in Sandy Hook—

Sometimes in class we sit in a circle and people talk about their efforts to manage chronic pain and depression and anger. One guy tells an anecdote about an episode of road rage, which dissipated when he realized the other driver was a beautiful woman.

—

In the hot tub at the Y tonight—my hips are aching. A woman climbs down the stairs into the water and wades toward me, smiling. I've seen her many times in this locker room, but we've never spoken.

"Hello," I say. "How are you tonight?"

"I'm celebrating! A birthday, a book, a lifetime. Praise Jesus. Can you guess how old I am?"

"Well that's a trick question if I ever heard one. Sixty?"

"You know black don't crack! I'm seventy years old. And for forty years I've had my own catering business. I just published a book about my life in the food industry. My friends threw me a party at Scott's. Look me up on Facebook and you can see the pictures."

"You're a writer? Me too."

She has the most beautiful eyes and dimples. Like Vee, and like my sister. They'll all be pretty girls until the day they die.

She tells me about her granddaughter who just had successful bariatric surgery. "She takes after me, but it took me a *long* time to get this big. She did it by the time she was sixteen." She talks about the food her parents ate growing up in Louisiana and the way kids eat now.

She says she wants to write another book.

"What about?" I ask.

"I'm calling it *The Mess in Christian Life.*

"I'm Linda," I say. "What's your name?"

"Reverend Esther, but you can call me Esther."

"Oh, where is your church?"

"Wherever I am. Wherever I am, that's where my church is."

"So we're in your church right now? In the water?"

She smiles and nods. I stand up straight and she squints and looks at my chest.

"That's a nice necklace," she says. "I like the beads. The color of water. But you know," she says, "I think you could be getting more out of them beads."

"I have to jump in the pool before it closes," I say, climbing out of the tub.

"Next I see you I will give you my book and you'll learn about my life."

After my swim I heard her calling my name in the locker room and I found her at the sinks.

"Oh you're still here," she said. "I thought you'd gone."

She opened a small velvet pouch and shook a tiny cross, an ankh, and a little boil of oil onto the counter. "I want to give you a blessing," she said.

"OK," I said, and she took my hand and rubbed some oil on the back of it and bowed her head.

A minute later she was back to business, wiping her hands with a paper towel and packing up.

"Thank you," I said. "What should I do now?"

"Whatever you have to do, baby."

It's always been like this for me in Oakland, from back in the day at Lois the Pie Queen till now—people praying over me and around me.

There must be two hundred tiny churches in East Oakland. In a driveway near Havenscourt I once saw a tool shed from Home Depot adorned with a cross. In this town, if you hear the call, you can start a church (or be a writer).

2013

Mamamamamama

After meditation classes ended, I thought I might try going to Sunday Mass for several weeks in a row. I call myself an ex-Catholic, not a lapsed one, but I still cross myself at news of the unspeakable. The gesture and the rituals are encoded in me. I used to go to daily Mass in college before I lost my faith—that was my meditation practice, I guess.

So I've been going to St. Michael's, a black parish in West Oakland. Harry knows the pastor there, a black Jesuit who used to teach chemistry at Holy Cross. I decided I'd commit to three weeks in a row and see what happened.

Marcus came to Mass with me this week—arrived late, caused a bit of commotion, and sat down next to me.

He whispered in my ear: "I couldn't find this place at first. I went into a Korean church and I told them, 'I'm looking for my mom, Linda.' 'No Linda! No Linda!' They practically pushed me out the door."

Marcus had never been in a Catholic church. He looked at the people in the pew in front of us. They had a kneeler—we didn't.

"Why do they get a foot rest and we don't?" he said resentfully.

"That's not a foot rest, that's a kneeler. Shhh."

Marcus whispered running commentary, not paying attention to Greg (Fr. Charles; but I can't call any priest "Father" anymore). The priest glared at him, inspired, as he sermonized about sin and sex.

I whispered to Marcus, "Show respect and listen to him. I hear he has a PhD in chemistry."

"Well, I guess you have time for that kind of stuff if you're not getting laid."

I suppressed a laugh.

After Mass we drove over to a crumbling wall near West Oakland BART where he tagged last week. His tag, JOOS, in enormous blue letters.

—

This Sunday Greg started his sermon by mocking a girl who'd come to a memorial last week in those outrageously high heels everyone wears these days. He impersonated her tottering up to Communion, proud of herself, and I was embarrassed for all of us. The cruelty, the misogyny—so familiar. I looked around at the other parishioners. A few were laughing along.

I left before Communion.

So isn't this funny: I decide to go to Sunday Mass for three weeks in a row for the first time in thirty years, and the right-wing Pope resigns. Big news! First time a pope has resigned since fourteen something something.

Co-incidence? I don't think so.

—

I'm both shocking and too easily shocked—my faith and my doubt—purity and profanity—my contradictions—and my love for my friends who are converts—how do I explain myself?

> *You began Catholic, that is to say you began with a system of values in stark opposition to reality. Your mental existence is obsessed by a monstrous system of contradictions. You really believe in chastity, purity and the personal God and that is why you are always breaking out into cries of cunt, shit and hell.*
>
> H. G. Wells to James Joyce

—

Two weeks ago Richard called and needed money. I sent him $50 in cash. Didn't hear from him, so I called to see if he got it. "Yes," he said.

"Can you do something for me?" I asked.

"What?"

"Can you go light a candle for me at church?"

"Yeah, I can go to Arch Street, but now they have electric candles there. You want wax and a real flame?"

"Yes," I said. "That's what I want."

"OK, I'll see if I can go to St. John the Lesser. I think they still have real candles there."

206

Getting Isabel ready for college and for her surgery. I do it all myself, staying away from Andrew and his family. Too complicated, too painful, and they don't have time for it.

The co-parenting thing we managed for so many years has ended. Isabel doesn't want to spend much time there. It's simpler for me to do everything for and with her right now. And I don't mind giving up my swimming and my writing. She'll be gone soon and then I'll have too much time to myself.

We walk along Lakeshore and she takes my arm and we talk. Other mothers comment on our closeness. Kay said, "She never texts while she's with you? That's remarkable."

She's so beautiful. I see men looking at her in the street and in the store when we go grocery shopping. She's my replacement, in the grand scheme. I have become that Fellini character who fascinated Mastroianni's character in *8½*—that middle-aged woman in the background, thick around the waist, making her way down a slope in bare feet and black dress. A Maria.

—

Richard called at least twenty times yesterday, the day before a job review that promises to be hard because I want to ask for something: If they'd give me full-time work I could pay down my debt (but I'd have no time to write). I let the phone go to voicemail all day. But finally, just before I went to bed, I answered. He needs $700 right away. "I don't have it," I said, and he started in, filled with contempt for me, one of the "conventional people."

Then he began one of his monologues.

I tried to get a word in, to remind him that I'd sent him money not long ago. He told me that he was "not impressed" with the amount. Then he hung up on me.

—

I had brunch with Jackie last week when she came up from Los Angeles. She managed to get out of our mess of a workplace and is writing comedy screenplays and going to film school.

"How's my Isabel," she asked.

Isabel's portrait of Jackie is on Jackie's web site. "The Black female David Sedaris," Jackie bills herself (with his permission).

"She's fine. She's getting ready to apply to college."

My friendship with Jackie is much nicer than it was when we worked together in that office fraught with politics.

"I'm much more mellow now," she says. "Probably because of Buddhism."

"Me, too, probably because I no longer have my period or PMS."

She's having no luck with online dating but still has hope.

"I'd go out with an old white man or a young one. I'll try anything. I can see myself being a stepmother, I can practically write the pilot for the series. But you know what I want? I want what all black women want. I want to be cherished."

I don't say, "I know," because I can't presume to know. But she expects me to understand as best I can. That's why she's telling me.

———

In Boston to visit Bill and Fanny. The streets were icy, my boots were soaked. We took a cab from Cambridge to the South End with Rae. I'd never met her before. The driver was a white guy about my age. I told him my brother was also a cab driver in Boston. "A white guy? No way!" He looked at me in the rearview mirror. "There are only three or four white guys still driving cabs in Boston. I must know him. What's his name?"

I tell him, but he doesn't recognize the name. As we pay him and get out of the cab, I can hear him whispering incredulously to the dispatcher: "Have you ever heard of a Richard Norton?"

—

I leave the Woodberry Room to meet Bill for dinner. It's dark and snowing sleet.

When I was 23 I met Andrew here in Harvard Square at the bookstore where we worked shit shifts, six to midnight every Friday and Saturday. Too cool for me, I thought. But he persisted. One night I was sitting on a ladder at the back of the store, shelving books and reading Jane Bowles for the very first time. I had just finished her short story, "Everything is Nice," when he came around the corner, looked up at me, and read aloud: "Once upon a time and a very good time it was there was moocow coming down along the road." And: "When you wet the bed first it is warm then it gets cold." Then he told me he'd found five dollars on the ground during his break and asked me if I wanted to go to the Wursthaus for a drink with him after work.

I'd been obsessed with Dubliners *and* Portrait of the Artist *in college. Joyce was the first author I'd ever read who wrote about something like my life—Irish life, Catholic life. Surrounded by Jesuits and Irish boys, I read about a young man declaring himself the conscience of his race.*

But could a young woman artist ever be so presumptuous? Could a girl be the conscience of her race? And what was my race?

—

One night in Andrew's bed, I dreamed I was peeing in a toilet, and suddenly I woke up, realizing I'd actually pissed myself. I was horrified. But Andrew was totally cool about it. I read it as compassion, then, but maybe it was just a sign of his laissez faire approach to almost everything.

From Andrew I learned about art history and painting, including the word "odalisque." (He told me I was one.)

His roommates were dating townies with accents like mine when I met him; slumming. They soon dropped those girls and moved on to women with money and status, women more like them. Andrew married his townie.

Those few years—from 1984 when I moved to New Haven, to 1986, when Joey died—were the happiest years of my life before Isabel was born in 1994.

———

Now, thirty years later, my book is in the window of the Harvard Bookstore. I'm an ex-daughter, an ex-wife. And I'm smiling, though I'm freezing cold.

"The record is not over yet. The record is not over yet. The record is not over yet."—My last summer with Isabel before she leaves for college—Thank God I am writing again. I'll pour myself into it when she's gone.

My life is better since I swore off men. But sometimes I still find myself hoping to see Johnnie. I look for his car, I look for his face. It's been almost a year since I saw him last.

Today he was coming down the stairs of the gym as I was going up.

"I'm so glad to see you," I said. "Where have you been?"

He shook his head—no answer—and asked me about myself.

So much has changed in my life since I first met him. I gave up on men, published a book, traveled to give readings, learned to speak up, helped my daughter to adjust to her new family and health problems, and moved us into a new apartment. I'm older, and the woman I was, the one who dressed for him, is gone. But I didn't tell him all of that. I just talked about Isabel, who is going off to college soon.

Again I asked, "Where have you been? How are you?"

"Oh, I been awful sick. On my back at Kaiser Hayward for five months."

He used to keep his hair close-shaven but it's grown out a bit and it's white. He's gaunt and pale. I put my hand on his arm, cautiously; I've always been careful about touching him or even standing too close to him in public. He still has those biceps.

"What's wrong?"

He describes a condition with his esophagus and I realize, but dimly, that it's something that only happens to people who are HIV positive. Like the cytomegalovirus and pneumocystis that killed my brother.

But they can treat this kind of stuff now, right?

We stand there, catching up. There's no tension, no guilt. Some sadness mixed in with stoicism.

"Goodbye," I say. As I walk up the stairs I hear him call my name, and I turn around.

He looks at me with narrowed eyes, as if facing a harsh light.

"Yes?"

"You're still beautiful, you know."

—

Went home to Isabel after my encounter with Johnnie and a quick swim. I stretched on the floor on my mat in the parlor and she sat on the couch.

I said, "Do you remember Johnnie? You met him when you were younger—we were on the way to a bat mitzvah."

"I don't remember."

"I just ran into him at the Y." I reached for her ankle. "Did you ever know I loved him?"

She looked quizzical. She's never heard me say that about a man.

I told her a little about Johnnie's work, his hat, his car. His humility and his cockiness. But really I was talking to myself.

"Marcus came into my life," I said, "because of Johnnie."

Now she was standing up on the couch, looking down at me, smiling.

"You know," I said, "I sometimes think of Johnnie as Marcus's father. Johnnie would have been a good father."

At that she jumped off the couch, half-landed on me, and hugged me hard.

"Aargh!" I yelled. "'My best friend is trying to kill me!'" (My favorite line from *Frog and Toad*.)

We laughed and wrestled and rolled around, gasping for air and laughing.

—

My last day with Isabel in Portland before she starts college. Lou Reed's "It's Such a Perfect Day" came on the radio as we finished our goodbye lunch, and I gave her money to go up to the counter and pay the check. I didn't want her to see me cry. Otherwise I kept my composure. Until I got to the Portland airport. I hadn't eaten much of my lunch and I thought I should get a sandwich for the plane. But I couldn't figure out what to get. The girl at the counter offered to help me choose a sandwich.

I said, "You know, I feel like I just have to tell someone that I'm a single mother and I just dropped my only daughter off here for freshman year of college."

She said, "Oh no! My mom is single too and we're so close. I can't leave her, I decided to go to a junior college and commute. I love her so much!"

She burst out crying and so did I.

"Poor us," I said, hugging her. "Lucky us."

—

I've never really been alone, though I've often been lonely. This is the first time in my life that I can do what I want without thinking of, and caring for, other people.

I do still care for Isabel, of course, but from afar. Mothering by phone is like trying to cook from another room when you can't see or touch the pots.

—

Was feeling out of touch, so lonely for Isabel now that she's away at college, so I called her in the middle of the day. She was in bio lab. She said, "I was just thinking about you." I said, "What were you thinking?" She said, "Mamamamamamamama."

—

Went to meet Marcus at the BBQ place where he works (it's called Perdition). The dishwasher greeted me with a smile and told a waiter, "That's Marcus's mom."

I am?

"He's in the freezer," said the waiter, and turned to walk me to the back.

"Oh, I know where it is," I said, and went down the corridor and opened the door of the meat locker.

He was in there with all the carcasses. "Look," he says, showing me a cow skull. "I'm gonna dry it till all the meat falls off and then I'm gonna paint it."

"Come out, it's so cold. Let's eat."

We went next door and talked about this week in policing. He tells me about a cousin of his grandmother or a great-uncle or someone in the family way back when who did the impossible—killed a police officer in self-defense and got away with it.

The stuff of legend?

"No," he says, "it really happened!"

Then he tells me about a time someone shot him.

"So we're in the recycle place in Oakland and there's this little white kid, and he sees me, and next he's going crazy, digging through all the bins, all the junk, and finally he finds it, like he always knew it would be there: a little plastic toy gun. And I'm just sitting there minding my own business, and this kid comes over and points the gun in my face, and bang!"

—

I drove him home, past the crumbling wall near West Oakland BART where he tagged last week.

"Why is JOOS your tag?"

"You know—JOOS. Like O. J."

He looked at me, puzzled—how could I not know—after all this time?

"JOOS like Juice? Like O.J. Simpson?"

"Yeah."

Of course. Why hadn't I thought of that?

Because I'm white, I had forgotten that O. J. was a hero to many.

That day when O. J. led the police on the Bronco chase in LA., I was on a business trip, sitting at the bar of the Tabard Inn, drinking ginger ale. Everyone was staring at the TV. I didn't understand what the big deal was.

Marcus was five when Simpson did the impossible and beat the system.

Now I tell him about O. J. in the Hertz commercials. Back when O. J. was lighter. He doesn't know about that part of Simpson's life.

In the car a few years ago, on the way home from a court date, he read me a poem he wrote: "Since I was nine / I have been an immense black man / to everyone I see."

—

In New York for a reading of Pressed Wafer authors. Went up to 125th and bought a black slip at H&M and had an over-priced lunch at a place where the eggs tasted like disinfectant. Then on to the Schomburg where, years ago, I worked on the Marcus Garvey papers. I visited an exhibit of WPA photos and eavesdropped. I left as it was getting dark. I'd heard that Harlem had become gentrified and white, but I saw very few white people up there. The trees were bare and I had all the haunting feelings about architecture and oncoming winter that I had when I lived here. Feelings I don't have in California.

I stopped at Goodwill and found a snow globe of the Statue of Liberty with her head knocked off. I was "mesmotized," as my mother would say, shaking the thing and watching the snow swirl. But I didn't have time to wait in line to buy it. On the way to the subway, on a block of brownstones where I was the only soul in the street, a black cat crossed my path. For me, in Harlem, I thought, that might augur good luck.

—

A Christmas present: An email from someone I don't know, Alice, a poet and curator in Ireland. She read my book and loved it and writes so beautifully about it. We correspond as if we've known each other forever. We have so much in common. She invites me to come to Ireland. I say, "I'd love to, but I have no money." Someday, maybe.

—

Had a little party for Isabel and invited Andrew and family. Everyone wants me to be part of the family. They plunk the kids right down in my lap and expect me to do the right thing—to love. But it's hard. Unless we're playing. Then I just laugh, and I forget to be resentful.

—

Steve stopped by to say hello to Isabel. He noticed a scribbled quote from Bob Kaufman taped up over my desk.

"'Hoping the beat is really the truth.' I remember that you used it as an epigraph to your Strayhorn poems in *Shuffle Boil*," he said.

"Yeah, I've had that Post-It for a long time, since 2001. Lost so much, but

I kept that."

"Remember Julian from that night with Fred? He knows a lot about Kaufman. You should talk to him."

We had all gone out to dinner after Fred's talk about *Twelve Years a Slave*.

I still haven't answered the message Julian sent me right after we met. But I would like to hear what he has to say about Kaufman.

2014

Black Valley / Whiteface

New Year's Day. Another letter from Alice. She looked at my blog and saw my collages. Suggests I have a show at the Dock in Leitrim, where she's a curator. She will work on getting funding. "My God, yes," I say. That would be a dream come true. Where is Leitrim? I look at the map. Oh, it's near Roscommon, where my father's foster mother was born. And it's McGahern and Healy country. Some of my favorite writers.

How far is it from Kerry? I've only been to Ireland once, long ago, and just to Dublin.

—

"Heavy Arm" and "Breakout"—games I invented for Isabel—my contributions to the world of wild rumpus. Now I play these games with Andrew's other children, Isabel's little brother and sister. And Andrew's wife watches indulgently, excited about our "blended" family. This is what she envisioned. She has all my best qualities and so much more. She wants her kids to love me and they do. And she's good to Isabel.

I don't know if I can bear this. Sometimes I go home and cry. How did he end up with a family and home? How did I end up alone?

When will these kids realize that I was once married to their daddy?

—

Baldwin: "It was only when her purity ended that her life could begin."

Me: The dream of a male protector outlives all men.

—

What about your current self would most surprise the girl you were?

Pretty much everything.

—

My notebooks, filled with memories of my parents—from the very beginning, it seems, the thing that interested me most was documenting them, trying to understand them.

—

My father banging the side of his pipe against the porcelain toilet bowl—there were always tobacco flakes in the water—but if he saw evidence of my menstrual blood in the bathroom: Disgust and shame.

And him sitting on the back steps in the dark on summer nights, listening to the Red Sox game on the transistor radio; his absolute loneliness, as if he weren't a member of our family, and didn't want to be—because he had his beer and his God—and didn't like us much.

And, at the beach, him running out into the water and crossing himself before diving into the waves. How tall and athletic and freckled he was.

And Ma's little Avon lipstick sampler—the aqua plastic box—with tiny lipsticks—she kept the box in the refrigerator in summer so they wouldn't melt. I thought then that I'd like a job where you name things—lipsticks, streets, roses.

"On the Street Where You Live," the song that played on the music box in which she kept her jewelry.

And that time in 1969 when the boys complained that the potatoes were still kinda raw on our plates, and she said, "Ever since those men went to the moon, the potatoes don't cook like they used to."

I drove to Marin to visit with Corrine. And she's so in love, so happy. We sat on the terrace and she beamed in the sunshine. She *looks* loved. She's written the most beautiful book of poems out of this late-life, seemingly doomed affair. I'd like to have a muse—to be in love. I'd like to write love poems.

—

Letter from Alice in Ireland. She got funding for a show of my collages in Ireland in the fall of 2014. I'm in shock. Better start making more work. I'm going to call the show "Dark White."

—

At Half-Price Books I found a catalogue filled with things to use in my collages, *The Conflict as Seen Through Collectibles*, a book about Vietnam War paraphernalia, including things a military chaplain or rabbi needs in order to conduct funerals in the jungle.

—

Painting at my desk. Scratching away at the surface, trying to complicate it. Then I cut, pasted, and painted late into the night, forgetting, for hours on end, to take a sip—so focused that I accidentally dipped my brush in wine.

Lots of paintings must have some wine on them.

—

I pull out my files about my father's mother, Christie Sullivan and her mother, Mary Kissane Sullivan, and read once again the welfare report about my grandmother's case in 1932 and my father's infancy.

"Mother in again today," the social worker wrote. "Nicely dressed and in her same defiant mood."

Someday I'm going to write a book about her and her mother and me and shame and happiness and nerve and defiance. Maybe something called *How I Became Linda Norton*. A book about saving your own life.

—

I have small squares of canvas all over my apartment and I'm cutting, pasting, painting, varnishing. Looks like I'll have fifty pieces ready for the show in the fall.

I've started a separate notebook for the Irish trip. I'm terrified. It's been twenty years since I went to Europe. I've never had the time or money, and wasn't willing or able to leave Isabel for more than six days at a time. Now I'll be an ocean away from her.

—

Dublin, Carrick-on-Shannon, Limerick, Kerry, and then back to Dublin. I took trains everywhere and biked forty miles to my grandmother's part of the country in the Black Valley. And I visited St. Finian's asylum, the place where my great-grandmother died. And felt at home and at peace. And met the most wonderful people. Filled up two notebooks.

Now, back in Oakland, back to my old notebook. Already scheming about my next journey.

—

At second-hand bookstore on Piedmont Ave:

"Do you have any books by bell hooks?"

"Who?"

"bell hooks."

"Who's she?"

"Black. Feminist. Buddhist. Women's studies."

"Oh she could be anywhere. People beyond category are dispersed."

He gestures to the shelves and goes back to texting.

I walk down the block and wander into another store. I don't touch anything because I don't want to want anything. I just look and listen.

"Is this a hand-painted tablecloth?" a customer asks.

"I don't know," says the girl at the cash register. "But it's from India, where people do all kinds of outrageous things by hand."

—

"So the loss keeps changing its shape" — Hilary Mantel in a *New York Times* profile

"Scar as archive" — Brian Teare

—

Terrible headache. Went to the gym anyway.

Roxanne, my pal the evangelist, stops to proselytize me while I'm showering.

Her eyes glitter as she talks about Christ's suffering on the Cross. "Pastor says it was even worse than it was portrayed in the Passion of Christ," she says happily.

I go into the sauna and close my eyes. On the benches around me four women are talking and I think I hear one of them say, in the midst of a rapid-fire burst of talk: "When I was in Dachau." But then I realize they're speaking Chinese.

Putting on my makeup, my foundation at the counter at the gym, it looks like I'm rubbing whiteface on my cheeks and forehead.

Am I having a migraine? I'm hearing voices:

"Do you ever have 'lyric episodes'?"

"Like small strokes?"

Yes, if I'm lucky.

The Burnt Lands

1

> *What does that tattoo say*
> *That's my baby's name*
> *What is your baby's name*
> *UTOPIA*

—C. D. Wright, from "Body Language," *One Big Self*

I was invited to participate in an online project about the endless supply
of Black victims of police shootings. The organizer planned to commis-
sion a poem for every victim of police violence over the course of a sum-
mer. This was deadline poetry: you'd be given the name of the deceased
and asked to contribute a memorial to the web site within 24 hours of the
shooting. I wasn't sure about the project but I understood the impulse to
respond in an emergency, to acknowledge, to document. So I waited my
turn.

And then I forgot about it until, one night after a bad day at work, I
received an email with a name and a few details:

> *The deceased has been identified as Asshams Pharoah Manley, 30, of For-*
> *estville, Md., police said. The shooting happened around 11:20 p.m. when*
> *police say an officer went to investigate a car crash near Brooks Drive and*
> *Marlboro Pike. Police say Manley was running from the crash scene. . . .*
> *Police say Manley was shot during a struggle over the officer's gun. . . .*
> *After being shot, police say Manley continued to fight with the officer. A*
> *second officer arrived and deployed a Taser, but police say Manley was not*
> *restrained until a third officer arrived. . . . Manley was transported to a*
> *local hospital and police say tests were conducted to see if he was under the*
> *influence of an illegal substance. The test revealed that Manley had opiates*
> *and marijuana in his system, according to police.*

According to police.

Was there anyone to mourn him? If not, would his name disappear? And what was there to say? Or, more accurately, what was there for me to say? I'd read some of the well-intentioned poems on the memorial web site. Just to graze upon the dead—no.

Silence might be best. But bypassing the chance to note this life did not seem right.

Then I thought about that name—"Asshams." Muslims would know what that name meant, but I didn't. So I searched and found that "ash-Shams" was a sura of the Q'uran.

In the police report they'd messed up the spelling in his name, calling him "Asshams" so it read like "ass" and "hams." ("I want my ham," says the holy fool in an August Wilson play, searching everywhere for justice, for what was owed.)

The mother and father of the deceased had given him this name, or perhaps he had taken it upon himself during a conversion.

Now I thought about his middle name. Named after the great tenor saxophonist, Pharoah Sanders, or the pharaohs of Egypt?

And "Manley"—that was a slave name, probably. Maybe, if he had lived, the deceased would have taken the last name "X" or "Ali," or something else to go with As-shams, the way Cassius Clay and Malcolm Little changed their names. "Manley" was a name and also a word with a meaning. Like "Little." Like "Clay."

I went looking for the name Manley in the WPA oral histories of former slaves. They were very old people when their testimony was taken in 1936, the year my mother was born; not ancient history—living history. In me and all around me.

2

ash-Shams

This Surah, a chapter of the Q'uran, is named for
"ash-Shams," which means
"the Sun"
Its theme is to distinguish the good from the evil and to warn the people.
By the sun and its brightness
And by the moon when it follows it.
And by the day when it brightens it—
(When the most wretched of them got up)

Pharaoh

The earliest Pharaohs of Egypt were associated with the Greek gods
(Apollo, Aelos, Gaia, Ares, Zeus, Hermes). But there are gaps in the
record, so the correlations aren't always clear.

These legendary Gods are followed by semi-divine rulers.

The slave ships had names—*Mercy, Happy Returns, Blessings, Constant
Abigail*—

But the captured were nameless cargo, transported in chains from Benin
to North Carolina, then up to Maryland and re-named.

3

Manley

From WPA oral histories with former slaves, recorded during the
Great Depression, about seventy-five years after the Emancipation
Proclamation:

> *My mother was named Melinda Manley, the slave of Governor
> Manley of North Carolina, and my father was named Arnold
> Foreman, slave of Bob and John Foreman, two young masters. . . I
> didn't never stay with my mammy [during] slavery.*

Betty Chessier, enslaved in North Carolina

She never got to keep them. When her fourth baby was born and was about two months old she just [knew] she would have to give it up and one day she said, "I just decided I'm not going to let old Master sell this baby; he just ain't going to do it." She got up and give it something out of a bottle and purty soon it was dead. 'Course didn't nobody tell on her or he'd of beat her nearly to death.

Lou Smith, enslaved in South Carolina and Arkansas

I have a faint recollection of my grandparents. My grandfather was sold to a man in South Carolina, to work in the rice field. Grand-mother drowned herself in the river when she heard that grand-pap was going away. I was told that grandpap was sold because he got religious and prayed that God would set him and grandma free.

Mary James, enslaved in Virginia

4

Fire.
That is their way of lighting candles in the darkness.
A White Philosopher said
'It is better to light one candle than curse the darkness.'
    These candles curse—
inverting the deeps of the darkness.

     Gwendolyn Brooks, "The Third Sermon on The Warpland"

"Those questions?"
The sharp sword with two edges:
to degrade persons into
representatives of truths.
And the curious way we write

what we think, yet very faintly,
pure white amidst the fields
of pink ones in the burnt lands,
circumference without relief.
In the distance a great
white mass rose lazily.

What distinguishes them is what James
once described as a "holy stupidity."
I will write upon them the name of God.
If thou fill thy brain with Boston and New York,
gaslight and heater and aqueduct,
all voting is a sort of gaming.
The angels indeed consorted with
the daughters of men, the devils also:
how awkward at the hymn.

I find this view amazing:
the seven stars in his right hand,
their toys, the designs for wallpapers
or oilcloths or carpets, the opponents
of a reform in Massachusetts.
But you have your own hammock.
Split the lark.

If all this studying is going to prepare him
to be a porter or a bellboy,
the same at last and at last
when peace is declared,
I have a few things against thee.

Thus does the universe wear
our color and this country has more reason
to despair. As though a white man were
anything more dignified than a white-
washed negro. I went to school

but was not wise enough to know.

The hidden laws that really govern
this society, and made her doom
inevitable, she remembered
many a winter and summer.
A door was opened in the heavens
and the first voice I heard: the whistle
of the locomotive. As I walked away
I was full of thoughtfulness,
my residence within.

"You haven't seen the South yet."
But I saw four angels
tied in your mouth.
In mine they began to loosen.
Do I not know, do I
not know, do I not know
this is delicious evening when
the whole body is one sense?
In landlessness resides
the highest truth, shore-
less, indefinite as God.
The star's whole secret
is the lake.

The Klan reappeared
and I saw the seven angels.
You may read in many languages
and read nothing about it.
We are afraid of truth.
He says, "That's good."
I cannot demonstrate it
but it seems to me
that he leans against the grave
paralyzed with gold.

Beyond Category: Journals

2015

An Nóta Gorm

New Year's Day. Isabel left for a trip to Washington, DC, with her boyfriend. Andrew and family went on a luxury vacation in Mexico. I was so alone. Everyone I knew was out of town. It was freezing in the apartment so I built a fire. I didn't know what to do with myself. I had an urge to get rid of something—everything, really. I pulled my notebooks out of the cabinet and paged through them.

My journals, as far as my dating life goes, are like fieldwork notebooks, like anthropologist Michael Taussig's book, *I Swear I Saw This*. I could write sequels: "I Swear I Heard This" and "Incredible Things Men Actually Expected Me to Believe." And of course (perhaps a slimmer volume), "I Can't Fucking Believe I Did That."

I never wanted to know all the things I've learned about men. What to do with this knowledge, since it's all that I have now, and it was so hard won?

> *Adam notices that Eve is holding something close as they leave the garden. He asks her what she carries so carefully. She replies that it is a little of the apple core kept for their children.*

—From the autobiography of William Butler Yeats

I tore out pages, tossing them into the fire. How ridiculous, how pathetic, how much time I'd wasted. And how much fun I'd had.

But when I got to my notebooks from 2007, 2008, 2009, and found the things I'd written about Johnnie, I stopped throwing pages in the fire. That bit of foolishness, that dream, that nobility and tenderness and love—a tragicomedy "beyond category."

I hadn't seen him for so long. And he was sick. I knew he must be gone. But I couldn't bring myself to look into it. Too much loss, too much death. And he's not mine.

—

In another journal, I find my notes about a movie review by Zadie Smith: "The possible happiness of two people in love cannot justify the guaranteed unhappiness of other parties who may be injured—what some would call 'collateral damage.'"

———

I stirred the ashes and then I did what I have avoided doing for so long—I searched for Johnnie. And there it was—his obituary. He was 59. He died exactly one month after that black cat crossed my path in Harlem. Five months after I saw him last.

I always wondered if I'd see him again. Now I know I never will.

Three or four clicks—how strange and lonely and unseemly, this search—and I read all I'll ever know about Johnnie's wife.

From her comments under his online obituary I learn that she was in her own hospital bed in the ICU when he died elsewhere in the hospital after his long illness. She was so sick she couldn't leave her bed to bury him. She'd had three strokes and two heart attacks in the last ten years.

"So much has happened since he passed, but he has been with me every step of the way."

I hear her and my heart goes out to her. And then my heart comes back to its place—separate, private, alone.

Under Johnnie's obituary I find tributes from all kinds of people who knew Johnnie better than I did.

"So very Blessed to have known and worked with you."

"I met Johnnie in 1992 I was his counselor and friend I watched Johnnie grow and become the man that he became. This is a great loss."

"An inspiration who made a difference."

"We will miss you, Johnnie. You were a real soldier and never gave up the fight of helping others with grace and humor."

"He gave so much."

I think of his face and all the things he said to me—that day he told me, fiercely and out of the blue, as I was letting go: "You'll see, it's not over yet." Like he knew something I didn't know, something he couldn't actually say.

I shake all my notebooks to see what comes out. Isabel's report cards, ticket stubs, a eucalyptus leaf, and another DVD he gave me—something I'd forgotten. He was so proud of it. I play it and hear his rhymes—a kind of rap. He was a real poet. I hardly talked to him about my writing. There wasn't time. And, in those days, my writing was still kind of a secret.

I'll try to visit his grave in Richmond next week. And then maybe I'll watch, after all these years, the ending of *Gone, Baby, Gone* that we missed when we left the movie early that Friday long ago.

—

More killing and more protests and "riots" this week, here in Oakland and everywhere. I was going to meet Marcus near City Hall and eat at Xolo last night, but downtown the glass from shattered car windows (from the last protest) still glitters in the streets, and I can't risk damage to my car.

So I picked him up on West Street and we drove around slowly, watching the police setting up barricades. Then we went to my place and made spaghetti and listened to the helicopters hovering. I put flowers in vases. He sprinkled sugar in the water to make the flowers last longer. Something I never do. "Thank you."

I microwaved the bread pudding I made last week. Then we sat on the couch with my computer, looking at Yelp reviews and music videos. Next he showed me his friend's funny nude pictures on FB (oh no). Time to say goodnight.

Outside, on the front steps, we looked up at the helicopters that circle every time something happens in Oakland. Marcus took out his green laser beam and pointed at the stars.

I drove him back downtown and we talked about looting. Last year he told me that he'd grabbed some shoeboxes from a store on a night like this. I used to be shocked when I watched such scenes on the news. Now I don't see things the same way. I'm worried about him, not the property, and I hope he won't do it again. I don't want him to get hurt.

I dropped him at his place and he leaned into my window to kiss me. A police car sped past us with lights flashing.

"Bye," he said. "Look for me later on the news!"

I laughed.

"No. Go play a video game."

He waved and smiled as he walked away.

"I love you," he called out.

I waited for him to close his front door before I drove home through streets filled with police cars and barriers.

—

Last night I saw flashing lights and heard cops on a bullhorn telling residents (me and my neighbors) to stay inside because they'd released attack dogs that might bite us. They were searching for an armed suspect who'd just shot someone near the 12th Street BART station. Last weekend, I saw the former governor at the gym (he was grousing at someone who was trying to help him). On Tuesday, a handsome man who looked like Michael McClure almost crashed into my car as I was driving to work. The next day, at the highway exit on Telegraph, I saw a homeless man checking his day planner.

—

on my back porch

where I listen to train whistles and the drone of highway traffic

and look up at planes and stars

—

To Marcus's place on West Street to bring him spaghetti and brownies. Harrell was there. I had to pee so they went into the bathroom (they keep it sparkling clean) to jiggle the plumbing for me. I'm proud of Marcus for paying rent, for having a job and his own apartment and furnishing it with things he's picked up on the sidewalk and carried on his back—two dressers and two couches.

When I came back from the bathroom their pet lizard was walking across the hall. Marcus scooped it up and cuddled it.

He has a huge TV in his room. He showed me how you play his video game. "There are never any little kids in video games," he said. "So if you shoot someone in the head, you know it won't accidentally hit a baby in a stroller."

On the wall there were paintings he'd made, and a picture of Lil B, along with a few collages I'd given him and a note I'd sent him long ago.

He wanted to go to an anti-gentrification party at the people's park on San Pablo. I told him I didn't want to go—"I'll be the oldest person there by thirty years, I'm sure." But he insisted, so we drove over. They were barbecuing tofu and making vegan pizzas in the handmade stone oven and painting a mural that says "Afrikatown." He introduced me to everyone as his mom. No one batted an eye.

I wandered off to the tables staffed by tenants' rights advocates and I saw a couple I recognized—those people who took my bed off the street after I listed it on Craigslist. Now they have a baby.

I recognized a guy I know from campus, a student journalist. I had helped him with his Africana studies research in the library a few times in his freshman year. Since the murders of Michael Brown and Tamir Rice, I've read some of his work in a local Black paper. Now he's writing about separatism as the answer to the problems of our time and place. The problems that never go away in America.

He looked at me, more wary than friendly, and said, "Hey Linda." I was surprised he remembered my name.

Marcus stood nearby, talking about evictions with a volunteer lawyer and listening to every word. He notices and remembers everything; he could be a detective. He has scrutinized me from the very start. He seems to remember everything that I or anyone else has ever said to him. Now he scrutinizes everyone who talks to me.

"Hey, how are you?" I said to the guy from the library. I thought his name was Trey, but I wasn't sure. "Forgive me—remind me of your name?"

"Rashid," he said

Marcus tugged at my sleeve.

"Let's go. I'm bored. And I'm hungry."

"How can you be hungry?" I said. "You just ate a quart of spaghetti."

I introduced them. "This is Marcus. Marcus, Rashid." They nodded at each other.

"Gotta go," I said. "Nice to see you."

We walked toward the gate and the burrito shop. I said to Marcus, "You know, I think the last time I saw him his name was Trey."

"We're in Afrikatown," he said drily. "If we stayed five more minutes, you'd be Rashida."

—

At one point, for instance, I drove in the company of a black family for a good half an hour. They waved repeatedly to show that I already had a place in their hearts as a friend of the family, as it were, and when they parted from me in a broad curve at the Hurleyville exit—the children pulling clownish faces out of the rearview window—I felt deserted and desolate for a time. —W. G. Sebald, The Emigrants

Driving around Lake Merritt last Sunday I almost rear-ended the car in front of me when it stopped short at a light. I didn't beep the horn or anything, I wasn't mad; I was just grateful that I'd been paying attention. And I was curious. I pulled up alongside the car to get a better look.

In the front seat was an old Chinese man and in the back was a woman I took to be his wife. There were quince branches on the dashboard, branches pressed up against the glass of the windows, branches from floor to ceiling, branches all around their faces. The car was a battered grey sedan held together with duct tape, like my car.

These elderly people were entirely surrounded by spiny branches but they weren't shielding their eyes with their hands or driving carefully. It was as if only I could see the danger they were in.

—

Rae read my book, said "Trinity" reminded her of Plath. Huh, I never thought of that. In my twenties, in Cambridge, everyone talked about Plath and Sexton. Seemed like you'd have to kill yourself if you were a female poet. And what about their poor children?

Plath bit Ted Hughes the night they met—drew blood. I've gotten pretty crazy around some men, but I've never bitten any of them.

—

Walking on Broadway from BART on Saturday night, I saw two tall men walking toward me, smiling. One of them opened his arms wide, and I realized it was Marcus with Harrell.

I was so glad to see them. I let myself be enveloped.

"Where are you going?"

"To see Lil B." Marcus gestured toward the club.

"How are you, Harrell? What are you doing these days?"

"Mostly boxing."

"At that place near me? I should come down and watch you guys some time. Have you ever seen *Raging Bull*?" He shook his head. "That's my favorite movie. You always wear a helmet, right?" He nodded. "You have to take care of your brain. It's the most important thing you got."

"That and family," he said, smiling and bending down to hug me. They walked me to my car.

I drove home feeling grateful and scared. Scared for them, and scared for me, too.

What if Marcus decides someday that I'm not family?

That could happen.

—

In my old notebooks I find perhaps my favorite intimate interracial exchange in literature (not that there are so many of them, really)—an argument in Baldwin's *Another Country*—the black character calling out her white lover:

Ida: "You are just a fucked-up group of people!"

Vivaldo: "I am just a fucked-up group of people!"

What she says—and what he says—sound like things I would say in a fight.

—

I haven't yet found a character like me in literature, and that's why I keep notebooks—to document what Wayne Koestenbaum calls "consciousness as I have endured it" (or enjoyed it).

—

In Portland, sitting in the Reed College archives where Isabel is working this summer, reading Philip Whalen's senior thesis—*Calendar*, a selection of poems. "Sun in the bamboos / Beside the lake / The ducks behaving / Scandalously" (from "The Great Instauration").

I work in a similar place—a research institute within an archive in a research library—where I can read things like this—rare things, like the pamphlet from Baraka's talk in Boston in the 1970s—about why blacks and working-class Irish Americans should make common cause with each other.

—

My Airbnb host in Portland, a nice retired fellow, just injured his leg in a heavy metal band drumming accident in the basement.

On my walk to Powell's today I heard a man playing bagpipes in his house. The sound was very faint, filtered through a screen and leaves. Bought another volume of Ferrante. Everyone is reading her or Knausgaard these days.

So many strip clubs in this town. Great bread and lots of beer. So many poor white people living on the street.

—

I tried to help Isabel set up her new apartment, arranging spices and cereal and things. I found a lamp in the street and we put it on her desk. Then I concentrated on window locks, security, and lights so she won't be raped. At the same time, I tried to remind her to do what she wants, don't be afraid, etc. It's the kind of conversation I've been having with myself for forty years. Depressing.

Finished Maggie Nelson's *The Argonauts* and Dodie's *The Buddhist*. Why do I always tell it slant? Why can't I just put my sex life out there the way they do? I bought a red notebook and started writing furiously about my sexual history. Love, hate, eros, the ludic, the absurd—liner notes for my soundtrack. The way it was. I poured it all out. And now I realize that I lost the fucking notebook on the way home from Portland. I'm feeling like a middle-aged and vulnerable Harriet the Spy, because, most of all, my notebooks tell the truth about me, even when—especially when—I write most honestly about other people.

I texted Isabel to tell her that I was home.

Me: And I think I lost my red notebook.
Isabel: Oh no! Any idea where it got lost?
Me: Your room? If you find it, burn it. LOL
Isabel: Heh heh . . .
Me: Please don't read it if you find it.
Me: Just tuck it into Philip Whalen's thesis in the Reed archives.
Me: So someone finds it later and says, "WTF?"
Isabel: A little bit of parent Reediana
Isabel: Highly classified
Me: Please, please, please, if you find it
Me: Tag it "hella Oakland" before you archive it.

At PDX heading back to Oakland, hanging around in the bookstore, I realized I could no longer avoid Knausgaard's *My Struggle*, so I bought it.

But somehow I lost that, too, before I got home.

—

I got a grant for my writing and a community project in East Oakland. Interviews, art, working with kids, etc. Thank God. I would not be able to keep paying my rent without it.

I'm re-reading C. D. Wright and thinking about documentary poetry. I look at the website for the California prison system and make a long, long list poem—the names of all the facilities. Then I look up the facilities, and find that there are reviews of prisons on Yelp!

A found poem:

One Star

"The spirit of every age," writes Eric Schlosser, "is manifest in its public works." So this is who we are, the jailers, the jailed. This is the spirit of our age.

C. D. Wright, "Stripe for Stripe," *One Big Self*

Not exactly sure how to rate a prison. I am not an inmate.
I was visiting a long-time friend who is serving a life sentence.
Dress code: no yoga pants, underwire bras, no sleeveless shirts or
cleavage, no open-toe shoes. Do not wear orange, green, colors of
inmates' and guards' uniforms. There are vending machines. You can
even take a picture with inmate. The inmate cannot touch money so
please be advised. We had a great visit. I'll definitely go back.

•

I have an auntie that has spent almost 16 years in this place to date
LOL. Have been writing her and she calls me from time to time thru
out her time. There is always a lock down in there for the smallest
thing. We have been cut off of some phone calls bc of whatever going
on. From what I know about the place, it's just a big joke! There are
more addicts in there then on the streets bc drugs are constantly
brought in by guards. A lot of them are jeopardizing their job con-
stantly bc they get romantically involved with inmates. The place is a
big cesspool of constant drama! The place needs a revamp.

•

In the cell there was myself, three Mexican girls who got lost leaving
Modesto (???), a couple of black girls, and a couple of white girls. A
white girl asked to get switched to another cell because of the "she-
nanigans." "I'm with all these shenanigans! Can you put me with only
White people?" LOL!!!!! She then took all of the toilet paper to make
a blanket for herself. What fun, peeling layers from her every time I
needed to pee.

•

Can't EVEN believe there *ARE* jail Yelp reviews!!!! Even a moron
can predict what people are gonna say!!!! Are there any 5 stars jails in
existence???? LMFAO!!!!

•

Awful. Added one star for the arts and crafts program. I like macaroni pictures. What of it?

•

Protective custody inmates are mainly gang dropouts, chomos (child molesters/sex crimes), celebrities, people with high profile cases and LGBT status. These inmates wear red jail clothing. LGBT and sex crimes are housed with each other. People with mental disabilities and disorders unfortunately end up here too. These people get the shit end of the stick I'd say. I have been to Santa Rita more than three times and I have always witnessed deputies mocking and disrespecting mental individuals on several occasions. Mental inmates that are violent wear a distinctive jail suit consisting of green and white stripes and are always shackled with handcuffs and waist restraints. Whether your stay is overnight or extended, this place is for no person in their right mind.

Leaving can be bittersweet because you will find yourself making at least an acquaintance or two just by having them teach you the ropes. ENJOY :)

—

Working on my project about migration and incarceration in East Oakland. Doing interviews, making art with whoever comes in, and we made a little library in the community center. Angela Davis's books, Ruthie Gilmore's, Jarvis Jay Masters, and editions of Malcolm X for little kids, teenagers, and adults.

After our interview there last week, Beverly, about seventy-five years old and still beautiful in a picture hat and ballet slippers, sat with me on the porch talking about the things she wouldn't tell on tape. Remembered the dirty blues she liked when she was growing up in Texas. Things she did then that she wouldn't do now.

She mentioned a guy who came on to her in Home Depot years ago. He wanted to fix her sink, her electricity, her cabinets . . . It sounded like a poem, like the blues.

I was distracted and wasn't sure I was getting her meaning.

"Wait, was this guy white?"

She stared at me hard. "Well, he was a lot whiter than you are!"

———

Beverly tells the kids who come to my workshops that they should call me "Miss Linda" out of respect. I told them they could call me "Linda," but she wants to set a tone (they call her "Miss Beverly").

Jim, the nice old white donor and volunteer who's come to fix the porch, overhears this and looks puzzled. The kids call him Jim, or nothing at all.

He asks her, "Does that mean you want them to call me 'Mr. Jim'?"

Is it my imagination, or does he suddenly sound like his people came from Tennessee?

She says, "No. Oh, no no no no no no no."

"Why not?"

"Because of—history."

He looks puzzled. Beverly laughs and looks at me. "You wanna tell him?"

No, thanks. I don't want to tell Jim he looks like master. Jim is a really nice man.

The *helado* cart arrived in front of the park and a crowd gathered. Joss called me over to introduce me to some people, and I met a new baby named Nebulous. They handed her to me.

It was fabulous.

———

Last week, conducting a workshop with formerly incarcerated men in East Oakland. Felix, 30, killed a man with a punch to the head. Didn't mean to. Is on parole, trying to stay clean. He asked me, "Do you have a higher power?"

I shook my head. I didn't tell him that my grandmothers and their mothers are my higher power. That I want to vindicate their suffering with my life, my mothering, my happiness, my work.

—

On the news the talking heads are appalled, not by the murder of another unarmed black man by the police, but by *the looting*. I too used to think that looting and rioting was the real crime. But even when I was very young, I suspected that something worse was going on.

My uncle was a cop in Boston in the late 1960s. One Sunday at the kitchen table he showed us his bite mark from a riot.

The other adults shook their heads in sympathy. "Animals!" They were talking about "the Colored" again.

You didn't want to get too close to this uncle. He was scary and hairy, and he smelled. I thought he must have done something evil, like the policemen in the South, the ones you saw on TV, to get someone to bite him.

—

Exploring our library's trial subscription to the online edition of Harvard University Press's *Dictionary of American Regional English*, remembering being Sicilian in Boston. My Irish uncles called my mother a wop, like she was a filthy puppy. Like it was supposed to be funny. From the compendium of regional English, *Collier's* magazine, 1931: "I have a lot of very good friends among the Italians, and I never speak of them as wops, or guineas, or dagoes or grease balls."

—

Ash Wednesday. I remember putting Kleenex on my head if I forgot my hat or mantilla at church. I remember fish on Fridays.

I've always known what's wrong. It's taken me a lifetime to learn what's okay.

—

My birthday. I make a plan for friends to meet me at Brennan's. I invite Marcus and am a little surprised when he shows up. He came to my CCA lecture, too, and he spoke up. At Brennan's he bends down and puts his arms around me and rests his chin on the top of my head. Then sits next to me and suddenly these people begin to understand who he is to me.

He has a new haircut and new work shirt (with PERDITION embroidered on the pocket). He seems so comfortable with my friends. They're clearly dazzled by him.

We say goodnight and walk to my car. He puts his bike in my trunk so I can drive him home. Then he tells me everything he noticed about my friends and other people in the bar. Like Ma would say: "He don't miss a trick." I ask him about Mother's Day.

"Will you see your mother this year?"

"No, she's messed up."

We're quiet as we drive down San Pablo.

"You know," he says, "I'd really like to get her out of the ghetto for a day. Take her for a drive."

"Where would you take her?"

"Maybe to Vallejo. I hear they do Civil War battle reenactments there. I think it would do her good to see white people killing white people."

—

All Souls Day

Last night I dreamed Johnnie and I were at the lake where we used to see each other when I was riding past on my bike and he was out running. It was a sunny day but a flood came up and covered his car and his clothes, the things he loved. My stuff was on higher ground. I was worried about his things, but he wasn't. He acted like he had all the time in the world.

—

"And once again the fields of gloom are adroitly plowed under."

WOR radio announcer at the Savoy introducing Billie Holiday and Count Basie, circa 1935.

On Sundays I tune in to Billy's jazz show in Irish. Through the miracle of the Internet, he's broadcasting in Dublin and also here. "An Nóta Gorm," the show is called. "Blue Note" in Gaelic. Black Africans are called "fear gorm" in Irish—blue men—because "fear dubh"—black men—was already in use, from ancient times, to mean "the devil."

—

Long day editing yet another interview with yet another rich white man. I often feel like I'm a little seamstress—anonymously embroidering their dirty underwear (in an office directly above the vault where the papers of Eldridge Cleaver, Gwendolyn Brooks, and the Donner party are archived!).

Why do men talk and think about themselves in the third person as if they're gods or heroes? Is it because they have a thing they can look down on, a thing outside of themselves that grows and makes them marvel? "Look what he's doing now! See how big he gets!"

They're talking to themselves, not to us. They don't see us. They see their own reflections. We see through them.

2016

How Far Did You Get?

Looking for a sign—what to write—how to write it. The old problem: Do I have permission? And who cares what I think?

—

Every time I take the ferry I think it is the most beautiful thing that ever happened to me. The Port of Oakland, the beeping of the trucks backing up.

The dream, or is it a nightmare, where you forget to get off at your stop on the ferry from SF to Oakland and end up in East Boston.

—

The week before my friend Dan died, I sat with him in his apartment in the Mission. He told me he'd gone back to church for the sacrament of reconciliation—what we used to call confession. I said that I might do that, too, someday, if I could confess to a woman and not a priest.

A few months after he died, his wife held a memorial for him. It was in the Swedenborgian church where I'd been married, in Pacific Heights. I'd been anxious about possible emotional overload. Isabel surprised me by deciding, on her own, to come down for the weekend to attend the service with me.

On the way home, in the fog, as we drove past Fort Mason, she asked me, "What's the difference between a memorial and a funeral?"

Ah, she's so not Catholic.

"There's a body at a funeral."

Then I told her about wakes.

—

Marcus has been giving me piles of old photographs he finds in dumpsters—hundreds of snapshots and formal portraits of black people—strangers. I don't know what to do with them. This week I read an article by Teju Cole about found photos. "I had the sense that my possession of these pictures was not their ideal posterity." Me too. But now these things are my responsibility.

—

This morning at Trader Joe's I saw that stern-looking black Irishman from the gym, Johnnie's friend, whose name I still don't know. All these years and we've never said hello. In the store he was with a very dark-skinned woman who looked a little older than him. Her hair was short and grey and natural. They were standing right next to me, deciding on bread. Sour dough? Cracked wheat? He went off to get some boxed broth.

To speak or not to speak to her? I decided to follow my instinct.

I said, "Is that your husband?" She said yes. She was radiant, but not conventionally attractive. I hesitated. She smiled. I said, "I don't know your husband, but I always see him at the Y. And once, years ago, I heard another man say to him, 'You are a very lucky man,' and I always wondered about the woman they must have been talking about. And now I see it was you."

She took my hand. "Oh, that is so nice to hear. So nice. Yes, I feel lucky too."

I said, "Well, that was a little forward of me to say," and she said, "Oh, no, it's sweet," and smiled, and I went off to the frozen food aisle.

At the checkout line I saw them at the cash register. She glanced back at me and said something to him and smiled, and I saw a look on his face that I couldn't read. He walked toward me and took my hand. "Thank you so much for telling her that. Thank you so much." And then he hurried back to help her with the bags.

—

I stop in the next week at Andrew's house on the way home, because I'm lonely and because they all love me, despite or because.

I've been wondering when his kids would realize that there was a past when I lived with Daddy the way their mother now lives with Daddy. At their house last night I sat on the couch with the kids on either side of me, snuggling. I opened one of their books and turned the pages and read the dedication out loud. "What's a dedication?" Oliver asked. I explained. "I dedicated my book to your sister Isabel," I said.

Oliver said, "But not to Daddy?"

I said, "Well, Daddy's *in* the book."

This children's book was about mice. Good mice, bad mice, bad mice that turn out to be nice.

Soon we came to the word "regret."

Oliver was right on it. "What does that mean?"

I said, "It's something you feel when you're sorry—when you're sad about what you said or did. Or they're sad about what they said and did."

He says, "Is that why you and Daddy got unmarried?"

Ada nudged me. "Keep reading."

"I'll answer your questions some other time," I said to Oliver. "Or you can ask Daddy."

He leaned into me and twirled his finger in my necklace, tracing my cleavage absentmindedly while he listened to the rest of the story.

—

June 27th: A man is just a man but, as Toni Morrison put it, "A son? Now that's somebody." Happy birthday, Marcus. We had dinner and cake in the parlor and then we watched YouTube videos (O. J.'s 1978 Hertz commercial, which Marcus had never seen, and "Blackberry Molasses," a song he had told me he liked when he was little). Suddenly, from the window we heard Rosa on the landing reprimanding Sonia, the most strong-willed toddler I have ever known. Sonia's furiously angry about the birth of her baby sister. I hear her screaming about it every morning. Rosa's tone was controlled and gentle, as always, but her voice was shaking. We went downstairs to see what was going on.

"What happened?" I asked.

"I told Sonia she had to take her bath and before I knew it, she ran down the stairs and up the street."

Sonia was keeping an eye on me and Marcus and trying not to smile. Rosa was trying not to cry.

"There are cars and trucks in the street, Sonia," Rosa said. "The street can be so dangerous . . ."

She choked back a sob.

Marcus leaned forward and smiled conspiratorially at Sonia. He raised his hand to give her a high five. She wiped her eyes and smiled at me. I nodded.

She slapped his palm.

"Good job," he said. "How far did you get?"

Notes & Acknowledgments

All but one of the poems in this book were written between 2012 and 2016; for the most part, they are arranged here thematically, not chronologically, in a book that is otherwise a narrative of change over time.

"My Mary"—Everything but the title is from the Book of Job.

"My Mystic"—For Fanny Howe.

"Small Square"—Distributed as a broadside on the occasion of an exhibition and reading at the Dock Arts Centre, Carrick-on-Shannon, Co. Leitrim, Ireland, 2014.

"Begin in Blue"—Inspired by Laura Mullen's research at the Bancroft Library. This poem is for Bill Corbett.

"A Parakeet"—Originally published in my chapbook, *Hesitation Kit* (EtherDome, 2007; Colleen Lookingbill and Elizabeth Robinson, publishers). The epigraph and the quote that ends the poem are from Sylvia Townsend Warner's novel, *Lolly Willowes*.

"In My Girlish Days"—A song sung by Memphis Minnie (lyrics by Ernest Lawlers). Thank you to Donna De La Perriere for sharing the account that serves as epigraph.

"Coloratura"—A "found poem," inspired by a manual for voice coaches.

"Meditations in Another Emergency"—See Frank O'Hara's poem, "Meditations in an Emergency." "The awful consequence of perspective" comes from Joan Retallack's *The Poethical Wager*.

"Doll Values"— "My tiny, tiny my-ness" – Czeslaw Milosz.

"Book of" —From the Book of Job—one damaged page in a wet Bible I found in New Orleans' Lower Ninth Ward.

"My Little Brown Book" —For Fred Moten. That "elemental brown" is Emily Dickinson's. Those are George Lewis's "high dimples."

"(Angrily)" —Some stage directions from *A Raisin in the Sun*.

"Experience" —Written after reading Norman Fischer's book of essays of the same name.

"The Burnt Lands"—Parts one, two, and three: See Emory University's online database of the slave trade and the WPA oral histories of the formerly enslaved.

Part four: Each stanza contains a line from the poems of Emily Dickinson, the Book of Revelation, Herman Melville's *Moby Dick*, Henry David Thoreau's *Walden*, and essays by James Baldwin and Ralph Waldo Emerson.

"Narcotics cannot still the tooth": Emily Dickinson, #373

"Beyond category": Duke Ellington's highest form of praise for music and people he loved.

Poetry and prose in this book has been published, sometimes in different form, in these magazines and anthologies:

Hanging Loose
Berkeley Poetry Review
New American Writing
Occupoetry
Datableed
Fourteen Hills
Transfer
Ambush
Shuffle Boil / Amerarcana
Colorado Review
Eleven Eleven
Occasional Religion
Zen Monster
Spuyten Duyvil's 2017 anthology Resist Much /
Obey Little: Inaugural Poems to
the Resistance
Fish Anthology 2014 (Cork, Ireland)

Thanks to editors Paul Hoover, Maxine Chernoff, Steve Dickison, David Meltzer, Nick Whittington, Phillip Barron, Tavarez Ricardo, Bob Booker, Patrick Cahill, Esther Patterson, Stephanie G'Schwinde, Andrew David King, Hugh Behm-Steinberg, Denise Newman, Tyrone Williams, and Robert Hershon, Mark Pawlak, Dick Lourie, and Donna Brook.

Many people have read parts of this manuscript, or versions of it, and I have benefited from their feedback.

For critiques, hard questions, edits, inspiration and solidarity, thanks to Kathleen Cushman, Arthur Goldwag, Lynne Weiss, Cynde Ahart Wood, Beverly Crawford Ames, Julie Carr, Susan Moon, Naomi Schneider, Fanny Howe, Alice Lyons, and Valerie Curtis-Newton.

Dick Lourie at Hanging Loose Press saw a way I couldn't see. He inspired a major reorganization of this book in 2018 and then edited it with care and tact in 2019.

I'm also grateful to Katie Peterson, Rita Gaber, Leslie Larson, Shannon Monroe, Caroline Goodwin, Fred Moten, Craig Gilmore, Ruth Wilson Gilmore, John Keene, Evan Karp, Denise Leto, Harry Thomas, Shelly Bigams, Jackie Thornton, Bill Concannon, Jennifer Kerwin, Kathleen Fitzgerald; and to the late Dermot Healy, Bill Corbett, and C. D. Wright. Thanks also to everyone at SoundEye in Cork 2016, and to online readers of draft excerpts from *Wite Out*.

Cecil Giscombe, Clay Banes, Stan Mir, and Andrew David King were supportive when the prequel to this book, *The Public Gardens: Poems and History*, was published in 2011. I'm grateful for their faith in my work.

Thanks also to Frances Phillips and the Creative Work Fund, San Francisco State University (for a William Dickey Fellowship), the Tyrone Guthrie Centre in Annaghmakerrig, the Ucross Foundation and the Whiting Foundation Writer's Aid Program, Malcolm Marshall, New Day Jazz, *An Nóta Gorm*, the Oakland Public Library, the libraries at the University of California, Berkeley, and the Downtown Oakland YMCA.

Love to Bill (in memoriam), and Fanny, Alice, and Valerie. This book is for them.

 **Linda Norton** is the author of The Public Gardens: Poems and History, a finalist for a Los Angeles Times Book Prize, and two chapbooks. She is also a visual artist with a background in book publishing, oral history, and libraries and archives. She grew up in Boston, lived in Brooklyn for many years, and moved to California in 1995. A dual citizen of the US and Ireland/EU, she lives in Oakland.